Bard
Song

Bard
Song

Robin Herne

Winchester, UK
Washington, USA

First published by Moon Books, 2012
Moon Books is an imprint of John Hunt Publishing Ltd., Laurel House, Station Approach,
Alresford, Hants, SO24 9JH, UK
office1@o-books.net
www.o-books.com

For distributor details and how to order please visit the 'Ordering' section on our website.

Text copyright: Robin Herne 2008

ISBN: 978 1 78099 087 3

A CIP catalogue record for this book is available from the British Library.

Design: Stuart Davies

Printed in the UK by CPI Antony Rowe
Printed in the USA by Offset Paperback Mfrs, Inc

We operate a distinctive and ethical publishing philosophy in all
areas of our business, from our global network of authors to
production and worldwide distribution.

CONTENTS

The author would like to express his thanks to:

Patricia D. Taylor, a friend from my university days who first
encouraged me to try and publish my poetry;
James Parker, my other brother, for the suggestion of the title
(after I floundered for one);
To everyone in Clan Ogma, past and present, for enduring
years of my poetry in rituals;
Finally, to Brigantia herself, the fire of poetry, and to Ogmios,
the shaper of words.

Introduction

Poetry has been a passion of mine for many years, and is possibly one of the reasons behind (or maybe one of the consequences of) my relationship with Ogmios, the god of knowledge and eloquence reverenced by the tribes of Ancient Gaul and (I would argue on the basis of potty mystical visions, though currently without archaeological evidence to back them up) those of Britain and Ireland.

Almost all of the poetry you will find in this small book is metrical ~ some modern Pagans turn pale and run screaming for the hills at the thought of poetic metre (it smacks of discipline, structure, self-reflection and all those things that mortify the current inheritors of those ancient polytheists who built temples and astronomically-aligned stone circles, devised complex law-codes and laid the foundations of modern science, and did so many other things which require immense discipline, structure, and self-reflection). Poetry and ranting all in one book, what more could you ask?

I'm not railing against free verse or unstructured, spontaneous poetry. Blank verse can be very good, in the hands of an inspired wordsmith, though as often execrably bad in the pen of a doggerel-churner.

The mental focus gained from writing to structure, from editing one's own work to make the metaphor tighter, is (to use the drab jargon of the office) a transferable skill. The same focus is useful to meditation, trance induction, mediumship, and magic. Magic... now there's a word with a million meanings! In my previous book[1] one of the chapters explored the concept. For me, the notion of magic has very little to do with waving wands or conjuring rains of fire ~ it is more about the re-enchantment of the world. These days humanity seems to revel in the prosaic, bland and dreary... and then we wonder why large swathes of the country are depressed and medicated up to the eyeballs (or drunk, or drugged up on less legitimate substances). As Morris Berman has noted in his 1981 work *The Re-enchantment of the World*, our psychological landscape has changed dramatically in the last few centuries. Not so long ago people saw fairies round every corner, ghosts in each shadow, and wonderment in thunderstorms. There are still people who find life awe-inspiring and magical, but they are increasingly in the minority ~ or so it seems.

Berman writes about 'participating consciousness', the state of mind in which one feels part of the world, integral to it; this contrasts with the alienated mentality that sits at a distance and observes the world as something external to itself.

Magic perhaps is a word with too many confused meanings, and it may be better to talk of mysticism ~ except for many religions the mystical so often seems to involve a desire to get away from the world, an innate mistrust of the sensual. Within Druidry (of the sort that I follow, at least[2]) the mystical path is quite the opposite ~ an embrace of the sensual, a seeking of enlightenment in good food, music, sex, aroma etc. The material universe is the gateway to the transcendent, rather than a distraction from it. So many early British and Irish myths deal with shape shifting, underpinned by the notion of a soul flowing through many shapes and guises. To rediscover the beauty (and the terror) at the heart of existence, we must jump headlong into our physicality; be creatures of this world and not apart from it.

I have attended Wiccan, Druid, Heathen, Hellenic, Kemetic and other Pagan celebrations, and all the good ones have had certain key features in common ~ minds joined together and uplifted by such communal activities as chanting, singing and storytelling; the sharing of good food and drink; altered light conditions (candlelight, moonlight and so forth); a focus on external forces rather than self-obsession. Magic, in this sense, is about transforming the minds of the participants, keying them in to the glory of existence. The magic truly works if it endures beyond the ceremony. It's naïve to assume that we could permanently exist in a heightened state (for one thing, there'd be no-one left to work in supermarkets, causing Society to grind to a halt). however, if more of us could enjoy at least brief periods in which the world seemed a joy to live in, then there might be far fewer problems bedevilling our species.

Poetry is one of the windows into the realm of imagination, dream-images, passionate emotions, and spiritual awareness. It's not an ideal route for everyone, but for many writing their own or reading and listening to other people's words is a springboard to another level of reality.

As many polytheists (and other types of deist, for that matter) will realise already, writing poetry can be a form of sacrificial offering. It is a gift of words, a means of honouring and remembering the Gods, ancestors (especially those who evolved those metrical forms), other-than-human[3] entities, and the spirits of the land, sky and sea.

There are a wide variety of beliefs deposited under the banner of paganism, and the poetry presented here has been composed by a polytheist ~ someone (me, obviously) who is convinced of the existence of many deities, as real and independent beings. You don't have to share this belief to enjoy the poetry, but knowing my views might help you to understand it.

Writing poetry and reading it out before a potentially critical audience can also be a form of sacrifice (sometimes more for the listener than for the artist!) To offer poetry, prose, or dramatic writing to an audience is an exchange, a flow of ideas.

There is an irony about the decision to write metrical Irish and Welsh poetry as a sacrifice to Pagan Gods, which will not have been lost on any reader who has remained awake this far into the book. The Celtic metrical styles presented here are, of necessity, medieval ~ none of the poetic metres used in the Iron Age have survived in written form (though there is a slim possibility that some of those written down in the medieval period may have originated centuries earlier). In other words, most of these metrical forms were developed by Christian poets, and used mainly to praise Christ, the Virgin, the saints, and assorted Christian kings and dignitaries.

Why, you might well ask, would a polytheist want to use Christian metres to praise Pagan deities? Trust you to ask an awkward question! I could blither on about cultural continuity, the persistence of the *awen* across the ages, and all that guff ~ but the simpler answer is that I don't really know. I enjoy writing in and reading these metres, especially when composed by far better poets than me, and I find that the Gods and other spirits seem to warm to hearing these metres in ceremony. They like them, I like them, and thinking about the erratic theological context makes my three remaining brain cells ache.

Whilst in a maundering mood, there are features of Welsh and Irish poetry that do not work desperately well when the metres are being used to compose in the English language (something they were never originally intended to do, of course). For example, a passage from the *Auraicept na n-Eces* (The Scholar's Primer) advises on use of the *condaib*, a rhyming technique in which the rhyme is contingent on the vowel in one word having to be surrounded by the same number of consonants in the other word. For example, *pig* forms a *condaib* rhyme with *fig* (both being three letter words) but not with *swig* (because it has four letters). Whilst a modern English speaking poet could create *condaib* rhymes, the effort involved would not be warranted by the likelihood of the audience's appreciation.

Nearly all the poems appearing in this book were written for use in ritual, the first four chapters worth in Druid ceremonies that I have partaken in (mostly with my fellow Clan members). Some of the poems featured in Chapter Six were written to honour assorted deities from other cultural traditions, composed when I was invited to be a guest at Heathen *blótar*, or Hellenic and Roman ceremonies. Chapter Seven is a selection of humorous and nonsensical poems, to provide a bit of light relief.

Chapter Eight gives some instructions for those of you who might want to have a go at writing in some of the metres used in the book. The instructions are kept basic and, as any speaker of Welsh or Irish will notice immediately, are heavily Anglicised versions of the metres. The reason for this is that I am assuming most readers of this book will be English speakers for whom the complexities of Welsh or Irish pronunciations might prove too difficult for what is essentially an introductory tome.

Each chapter includes some reflection (not to say pompous and occasionally bombastic pontification) about the nature and usage of poetry within Irish and Welsh contexts, as well as a little background on the poems featured.

Most of the poetry in this book draws on Welsh and Irish mythical imagery. These cultures certainly have a rich heritage of verbal arts, and for many the notion of mystical poetry is almost synonymous with the Welsh bards and Irish *filid*.

Modern druidic Orders often discuss what the exact nature of a bard / *fili* is, and how it relates to 21st century life. One common question is whether a person can call him or herself a bard if they do not write poetry or engage in storytelling, music etc. Many Orders see the role as essentially about creativity, and so take the stance that if a person can bake cakes, carve marble blocks, or weave lovely macramé then they are indeed a Bard ~ even though they may be unable to string two rhymes together. If that is the policy of a given Order, then who am I to quibble? Well, who I am is a cantankerous old git who loves a good hard quibbling. Can I call myself a chef if I am incapable of cooking, but have a lovely singing voice[4]? Obviously such a self-defin-ition is somewhat pointless; a singer is a singer and not a chef. Likewise, a bard/*fili* is, by definition, someone who engages in poetry, storytelling, music and seership. If you can't do any of those things then there is very little point in calling yourself a bard or *fili*.

It seems to me that many of these appeals to broaden the definition of bard to mean "anyone even remotely creative" are underpinned by a world of psychological damage. It may possibly be true of all religions, but certainly the Pagan faiths seem to attract a lot of people in search of healing for the psycho-spiritual wounds inflicted on them by an inherently unhealthy society. In and of itself, there is nothing wrong with this ~ after all, providing healing and spiritual balance is a fundamental feature of just about every religion. However, there are those who seek to overcome their suffering and then there are those who just want to reinforce it.

A very common form of hang-up is the fear of exclusion, something that appears to be actively encouraged by a great many people in positions of leadership within the Pagan community (if the drearily repetitive hand-wringing about the imagined wickedness of elitism is anything to go by).

Suggesting that a person is not a bard can often be taken as some sort of terrible personal attack ~ an attempt to exclude them from a super club of which they deserve to be a member. Which, obviously, is codswallop. I cannot run a 4-minute mile, and I don't think any sports coach on earth could help me do so. Being told that I'm not a fast runner is, in no sense, a personal slur or an attempt to exclude me from sport. It is just a statement of fact, like pointing out that I'm not 6 feet tall or that I don't weight 19 stone[5]. Likewise, saying that a person who cannot dance can scarcely call herself a ballerina, or that one who cannot compose a poem is therefore not a bard is merely a factual statement based on the straight meaning of the words ~ rather than an attempt to bully or exclude. However, so many people within modern society seem to be constantly engaging in puerile attempts to redefine words in the desperate flight from anything that might (heaven forfend) hurt the feelings of a shrieking histrionic who, frankly, should get a grip that base intentions are impugned to anyone who will not kowtow.

Just because a person cannot write a poem does not mean they might not have amazing talents in some other area. It probably doesn't help that some Druid Orders have tiers, one of which is labelled Bard, through which people with no bardic talents whatsoever are meant to pass. In the ancient Insular Celtic and Gaulish worlds, there were various bodies of spiritual professionals ~ druids, bards, vates etc. Individuals within those historical groupings almost certainly specialised in specific skills, rather than trying to be Jacks-of-all-trades. Not everyone back then was likely expected to be artistic and master the poetic arts, so why expect it today?

Any discussion of poetry within a Druidic context cannot be complete without a mention of *awen* (or its Gaelic equivalent of *ai*, or *imbas*). Awen is mentioned throughout medieval (and therefore Christian) Welsh literature as a sort of poetic equivalent to the Holy Spirit, descending on bards and filling them with words and visions. Linguists think the word predates its Christian usage, and modern Pagans certainly claim it as their own.

Awen is a wild spirit, a passionate and consuming Muse that imparts not just pretty turns of phrase, but a new vision of the world. The *awenyddion* were medieval Welsh magician-poets, whose roots may well go back a long way, who spoke magical and prophetic verse whilst in trance. By the medieval period they would, of course, have been plying their arts within a Christian theological context. Whether they were mainstream in their beliefs or teetering on the edge of heresy is a matter for further research.

How much modern Pagan poetry is the product of such consuming force is debatable. As, indeed, is the necessity for it to be so ecstatically inspired. A poem composed sedately in the drawing room can say as much as a visionary one, and often be a lot easier for the reader to comprehend!

Poetry may express a spiritual vision, or equally may praise an admirable person, lampoon a venal one, record the history of a people, convey a moral lesson, be written purely for laughs, or serve any of a dozen other functions.

[1] *Old Gods, New Druids* published by 0 Books.

[2] A polytheist spirituality embracing the Gods and spirits of the land.

[3] A ghastly, clunking term currently in vogue for describing birds, beasts, trees, shrubbery, strange spirits and the like ~ anything with sapience that doesn't happen to be human.

[4] Anyone who has ever heard my atonal caterwauling knows this to be a lie!

[5] At least I'm not at the time of writing... and pray to all the Gods that I never will be, lest I end up as wide as I am tall!

## Chapter One

Samhain

The feast of the dead reminds me of two old Gaelic forms of poetry, the *forsundud* and the *ecnaire*. The *forsundud*, as described by Myles Dillon, was essentially a genealogical poem reciting the impressive lineage of noble lords and ladies. There are surviving examples, the earliest from the 7th century CE. These were not just lists of names, but included any claims to fame or social status worth bragging about. Even with these embellishments, they are not the most riveting of poetic forms for a 21st century reader. It is possible they may have been considered rather dull in their own day too ~ one of those 'worthy' aspects of elite culture that many upper- or middle-class people feel obliged to sit through in order to be seen as sophisticated.

Even though listening to a poetic family tree may have got a tad tedious at times, there are verses that hold interesting detail. An example, taken from the *Lebor Gabála Érenn* (a book of mythology relating tales of the Irish gods), of a verse concerning a famed person of yesteryear runs:

Ollamh Fódla, fierce in valour,
Marked out the Scholar's Rampart,
The first mighty king with grace
Who convened the Festival of Tara.

Fifty years, it was tuneful fame,
was he in the High Kingship over Ireland
so that from him, with fortunate freedom,
Ulaidh received its name.
He died a natural death within his capital

Ollamh Fódla was the king traditionally said to have organised the Brehon law codes, embodying Ireland's famed restorative justice system. Some commentators have speculated that he may be a euhemerised deity, perhaps the Dagda.

The poor may well have had their own *forsundud* too, which professional scribes never bothered committing to parchment. If they did engage in such art forms, doubtless they did so off their own bat rather than employing the prohibitively expensive services of a court poet. Not having any monarchs or abbots to brag of, they may well have imbued their tales with humour or sentiment rather than ambitious bragging, and probably made them all the more palatable for it.

Alternatively the poor may have stuck to the use of the *coronach*, the lamenting or keening song. The metrical form of such dirges is now uncertain, though the modern poet could draw inspiration from the work of Sir Walter Scott.

The reader could consider, if they have not already done so, composing their own *forsundud* to recite in honour of their ancestors at Samhain. Doing so may well involve conducting some research into one's own family, as there are surprisingly few people who know much about any generation beyond their grandparents. Actually, quite a few people don't even know much about the immediate waves of their kin ~ to do so may actually necessitate having to talk to their relatives!

The simple act of writing a poem can open up a whole can of corpse-eating worms. For those who are adopted, and have little or no knowledge of their blood kin, a *forsundud* can equally celebrate their adopted family. There are too many people around whose youth was bereft of a loving family, and were perhaps bounced around from one foster home to another without ever being anywhere long enough to bond. If, as an adult, you find a surrogate family composed of friends, then why not recall them and their lineage as part of your own?

Other people may well have had a family, but one in which

one or more immediate relatives behaved in so monstrous a way as to make the poet want to disown them. Can a praise-poem actually incorporate the incestuous father or violently alcoholic mother? Even the worst parent may have had brief lulls of kindness between the dark times, yet to gloss over the emotional and physical wounds may feel profoundly dishonest.

Many ancient cultures recognised two types of ancestor ~ the blessed, happy dead, and the dangerous, angry ghosts. The Romans had the feast of Lemuria in May to make offerings to the wrathful dead. These were the shades of peoples who could not rest either because they were suicides, or had been murdered, or had not received a decent funeral, or were just deeply unpleasant people in life. Making offerings to these tormented souls discouraged them from plaguing the living. The Egyptians also distinguished between the revered *Akhu* and the fearful, disconsolate *Muatu*.

Whilst specific terms from the Iron Age Druids have not survived, it is quite possible that they may also have distinguished between honourable and dishonourable (or at least disturbed) ancestors. Whether they had separate festivals for them, we can now only guess at. Our understanding of Celtic folklore is based upon stories recorded within the Christian period, wherein the shades of former days may sometimes have been seen through dark (rather than rosy) spectacles, or have been misinterpreted, or even simply forgotten about. The *sluagh* are seen now as somewhat grim, but it is difficult to know if they were always considered the angry dead.

Each of our ancestors has made a contribution, genetic or social, for good or ill, to what we are now. To blank out a person, even if they doubtless deserved it, may not be the most psychologically healthy approach. No more than is singing praise of someone you loathe. So, whilst we don't really know how black sheep may have been dealt with in historical praise poetry, it may be better for a modern Pagan to make honest mention, warts and all, of disliked relatives.

The *ecnaire* was another style of praise poem, specifically one to be read in honour of the departed at a funeral. Eulogies are difficult things to compose, as so often they lack honesty. These days we feel obliged to ladle the saccharine on with a trowel when speaking of the recently deceased, even if we had little nice to say about them in life. Though, equally, looking for the good in another person is no bad thing; even if, sometimes, one needs remarkably acute eyesight to find it.

A eulogy can be sung (and the *ecnaire* was intended to be put to music, not merely mumbled in embarrassed fashion from a pulpit) to a relative, a friend, a beloved pet. For that matter, one could sing such a thing over the ashes of the family home that burns down, or at the death of a favourite tree, or the end of a way of life. It is a poem of mourning, of transition, of seeking that which can be salvaged (a happy memory, a wise lesson etc) from a wrenching loss.

A popular motif in Irish and Welsh poetry was that of the old man or woman lamenting a golden youth, often the imagery of a land in winter being used to represent a life in its decline. Maybe the most famous example is Kuno Meyer's translation of the *Lament of the Old Woman of Beare*, in which an ancient goddess-like figure grieves for the good old days. The degree to which the external environment reflects the inner psychological state reflects something deeply rooted in the ancient, and hopefully modern, Pagan psyche.

The common practice today is to read a poem from a known poet, and there is nothing wrong in reading Auden's "*Stop all the clocks, cut off the telephone*", or whatever seems appropriate. It's much the same as an ancient lord paying the tribal bard to compose a few bewitching words for the funeral. Yet, to speak in your own voice, to think what you actually value and miss and wish you could still have... well, that can be at once healing and transforming, both for the grieving and for the dead. Ask Brighid. Actually, wait till the next chapter and then ask her!

The Dream of Óengus Óg - This first poem is based upon the myth of the romance between the god of love and the swan maiden Caer Ibormeith. Her surname means the yew berry (technically the yew does not have berries, but fleshy red arils ~ the only part of the tree which is not poisonous). The myth culminates at Samhain, a time of transition and change. Ever after the two lovers change at that festival, from swans to humans or back again. Most myths set at this time of year are rather gruesome, but this one is really quite sweet.

The Dream of Óengus Óg

Love is not pink, but bright red,
Aril bed, where lovers link
With chains of gold feather-light,
Mute white swan's wings safe enfold.

Four are my bright winged kisses,
That Man's mate misses, in spite
Of the kiss of her "Old Man" ~
How can he compare to This?

I am the heat of the heart,
That dare not part from the sweet
Recalled stroke of my pale wing,
Maids sing of how soul's veil broke.

Yet this cob was also reigned,
Gift gained made my own heart throb.
Silent she swam in my night,
Such a sight made my life dam.

Aisling ate my flesh, my mind
Obsessed, blind to all but Fate.

13

Moon-falls flame entranced, taunted,
Sun-tides haunted by "no name".

Spells could not call what words failed,
Song jailed in voiceless pen's thrall.
My own song reflected back,
Three years wrack midst joyful throng.

When the dream was made feather,
Unlinked tether crossed the stream,
Yet no bride price could be struck,
Scant luck ~ till her Way I tried.

I swallowed poison in Caer,
Yet the fire-fruit gave me joy.
My soul's plaintive cry she hushed,
Had I crushed her.... Can gods die?

The bitter seed passed on through,
Slow grew ~ its green veil grants need
Now, deathless testament tree
That all may see how We love.

White Raven's Brother - From Irish myth we move to Welsh, with the story of Brân the Blessed, the giant whose severed head for many years guarded the Isle of the Mighty against invasion. His name translates as raven, with sister Branwen being the white raven. Brân lost his head, and practically his entire family, at the end of a tumultuous battle with his Irish in-laws. The battle was sparked over the mistreatment of Branwen by her new husband and his courtiers, though it proved a futile affair for she died at the end of it anyway ~ her heart broken with grief.

The metre use here is a Welsh form called *cywydd llosgyrnog*, which was quite popular in the 13th and 14th centuries.

White Raven's Brother

Lake-born cauldron on brute's back borne,
Chief's shield to battle ogres sworn,
Twisting thorn, blood thirst to grasp hard.
Outraged lords forged an iron tomb,
To Wales they fled the too-hot room,
Bearing sword-cold womb to new guard.

Lake-eyed Brân whom no house could hold,
Took the cauldron worth more than gold,
Giant-kin told of their wild flight.
Turns the wheel till Ireland's king claims
Cauldron's wealth, Brân his brother blames ~
Dark deed shames the Island of Might.

Payment of golden fortune's horde
Salves no wounds, hands itch for the sword,
Cajole their Lord to shame his bride.
White Raven trains the starling wise,
Across the channel swift he flies,
Vengeance cries, Brân the sea bestrides.

Llyr's son scorns the waters decay,
Wades the bed of deep oceans grey,
Brooks no delay to sister's plea.
Alder's uncle bridges divides,
Craven wife-beaters he derides,
Time bides to squash this upstart flea.

Quarrelsome half-kin comes full turn,
Who lost the womb-bowl, slew young Gwern,
Did learn to break the gift he cost
His own heart split to see it done,

Brân robbed of sister, brother, son
Though war was won, near all was lost.

Pierced Thigh bleeding, Irish soil fed,
Five maids, seven men, all else dead,
"My Head now take, to lead your way",
These the dying words that Brân called
Though deep sorrow his kinsmen stalled,
Grief appalled, Britain's chief to slay.

The dead still speak to those with ears,
He cheered them through the vale of tears,
For eighty years the death-bird stayed
Till the door opened onto night,
The mountain king resumed his height,
And then beneath White Mount was laid.

There the Wondrous Head guarded well
Britain's shores ~ all invasions quell,
No plague befell our island nest
Till Arthur dug deep, took him hence
He alone to be our defence,
Scant sense ~ yet ravens never rest!

Gwynn's Guest - Written in *Tawddgyrch cadwynog* metre, this next poem is a response to the story in the Life of St Collen, wherein the saint received an invite from Gwynn app Nudd to visit him in his royal residence atop Glastonbury Tor. After much persuasion, the saint attended the feast and violated guest law by hurling holy water at the lord of the fairy hosts. It was written for a Samhain (or perhaps I should say *Gwyl Gaeaf*, to stick with the Welsh theme) festival in which we sang the praises of Gwynn, after whom my husky is named! The huntsman's own dog is called Dormath, which means 'death's door' and who rather echoes the Greek Cerberus (though, so far as I know, he has but one head).

Gwynn's Guest

Wind tears the Tor, unravels hair
Bound in plaits fair, wild blood yearning
For thunder's roar, this hill my Chair,
Blessed wolf's lair, white fire burning.

Tribes rise and fall, dank marsh tides flow,
Poor nuts do grow on such dank soil,
Hazel tree small, to ground crouched low
With pious woe, to "One God" loyal.

On this high land, my leave not sought,
This hermit caught, and summoned twice
Takes not the hand, guest-law counts naught
To saintly thought ~ yet comes at thrice!

Grand Collen climbs, fear his eye parts,
Sees fairy Arts ~ bold Gwynn's great Hall.
Fair wondrous times, bard song stirs hearts,
Dreams harp imparts (few hear the call.)

Bee-brewed mead gift fills the guest horn,
Soothes the careworn, the host's bond makes,
But all is rift ~ this monk thinks scorn
To toast the morn, dawn's dew thirst slakes.

Board groans with feast, succulent boar
Makes stomachs roar, yet the saint sneers,
His knife ungreased. "This food is poor,
Just leafs, no more!" Tree meat he fears.

Bondsmen bold garbed, to table tend,
Monk does not mend unmannered ways,
Casts comments barbed, his host to rend,
(I shall not bend, though the hound bays.)

"For men half-blue, I do not care",
False guest did swear, "Tis only Hell's
Dead, freezing hue that they half-wear."
Storm's shade does glare from Dormath's wells.

"Heaven's hope lost, for men half-red,
The burning dead ~ you demon horde!"
Such insults cost, my Branch had bled,
King's colour wed to lightning's sword.

Hazel little, his wisdom sparse,
Fast shifts his arse, fierce Dormath bays,
Old tree brittle, abandons farce,
Puts heel to grass, such churlish ways!

My Hall to mist, the veil down drawn,
Justice foresworn by Law of Hosts,
His trews saint pissed ~ such water-lorn
Scarce holy-born ~ thus his Faith toasts.

Too many Sidhe for hermit's taste,
No time to waste, he fled my Tor,
Telling tales twee, of how he faced
Wild Gwynn and chased me to Hell's door!

The Sky Tribe - Back to Irish myth, this poem recollects the tale
of King Conaire Mor whose mother was visited by a bird-man,
and who later encountered a whole flock of bird-men during his
adolescent adventures. This flock was under the leadership of the

war chief Nemglan, an intriguing character about whom no further references are made. Sadly little other mention can be found to these curious feathered beings, which put me in mind of an aerial equivalent to the sea-going selkies. Were these bird-people shapeshifters who wore feathered cloaks, like some Norse characters, or were they fixed into their hybrid shape?

The metre is a simplified variation on the *rannaigheacht mór*, one of my favourite ones to use (largely because it is so easy).

The Sky Tribe

Sky-borne, Danu's children came
In a great crow-cloud swirling,
This unwedded land to claim,
Embraced in wings unfurling.

Three days a fog of feathers
The once watchful hawk hooded.
Gifts for sparse land made tethers,
With seeds of tree lore wooded.

Summer's dawn chorused golden,
Dark mists dispersed, season new,
To Iron Mountain beholden
To the airts the bird-kin flew.

As seal may shed her soft skin,
And wolf peel back his warm pelt,
So may shift the brave bird-kin,
Their cloaks flesh to feather melt.

Bird-brained Fintan kept the tale
Of all seen from eyrie high,
But for him, a legend pale,

Lost without the hawk's sharp eye.

Lovers curl beneath swan's wing.
Whose gold chains make the heart light?
Bold Óengus and his aisling
Lift leaden lives to soul flight.

Conaire's wave-riders stripped,
Man-formed bold Nemglan's wise words
Forged the throne, from whence youth slipped,
In death borne by claws of birds.

Moon-blessed, star-touched holy glade,
Where the one-shaped sing to Gods,
Where the soul-sweet mead is made,
Invite us, the Tribe of Sky.

The House of Winter - Written in *Breccbairdne* metre, this short piece dwells upon death and the grave (known poetically in Scots Gaelic as the house of winter). It is really a nature poem, with only a brief reference to the mystical ~ in the form of the Old Woman, Cailleach who spreads winter as she leaves her cave, wherein she hibernates during the summer.

The House of Winter

Winter's House hungers,
Feeds on summer's hopelorn
Dreams, gifts unseized hueless
Fall to mulch, trees hardworn.

Mourners at summer's
Grave, grief-dulled words scatter
On dead ears, now spendthrift

With praise; mind's walls shatter.

The vain starve friendship,
Spend no love on fellows;
All but themselves forget,
Till winter makes fallow.

Dry wells are valued,
Their lost waters vaunted.
Harsh the Hag's cold vigil,
Late-won wisdom valid.

The Hag is giving,
Who but she is gifting
Second chances, golden,
To the foolish grifting?

Grandmother's snowfall
Lasts for but a season.
Death also thaws, springtide
Souls awake from Winter.

Rutting - Written in the somewhat terse *train rannaigechta moiré* metre, Rutting celebrates the season when the red deer get a good seeing to (if they are lucky). The less-lucky bucks tend to get gouged, or even killed, by the antlers of more rugged stags. The Gaelic name for November, *Damhir*, is also the word for rutting (and a rather rude term for the comparable human activity!)

Rutting

Antlers leaf-bare
Claw and clash bleak

21

Against the sky,
Stags cry and seek

Mates, life at death
Defiance roars
Nor meekly goes
As ice floes, hoar

Frosts murder by
Dawn, cold deeds done
At Hag's edict
The weak picked, run

On sleet-slick floors,
Doom assured yet
Not embraced till
Dance is still, let

The music lull;
Graveyard's pause, let
The harp be strung
Anew. Tongues set

Singing praise songs
To summers' dead
Though all is cold
Be bold, Stag bled

With lust's hot urge
In womb-dark seeds
Survive snow sleep
So weep not. Beads

On holly red

Cernunnos fair
Willing wove wreath
Antlers leaf-bare.

Chapter Two

Imbolc

In the introduction to the previous chapter I finished by mentioning Brighid, the goddess most intimately associated with the festival of Imbolc, and the concept that poetry can be healing and transforming.

Brigit is not so much a goddess as three related goddesses, sisters of the flame. One is the spirit of poetry, one that of black-smithing, and one of healing. Much can be gained from meditating on this image of the Triple Brighid, and the connections between these crafts and the nature of fire itself. The older figure of Brigantia also held sway as a guardian of the flocks and farmsteads.

As someone who has conducted ritual to and with Brighid, I would like to suggest that central to all three sisters is the focus of the hearth fire. She is very much a deity of the homestead and all that is important to the smooth running of a happy and productive rural home. In this regards she may be thought of as having a kinship with Hestia and Vesta in the Classical pantheons, and the High Wife of Heathen myth.

Though not specifically allied to poetry, the Irish concept of *imbas* is the quest for spiritual enlightenment. One might consider the fiery Brighid as a goddess who may well bring such spiritual enlightenment. There might seem to be a contradiction between spiritual enlightenment and domesticity, though I do not consider there to be one. In some cultures the spiritually minded become mendicants and eschew the simple pleasures of a comfortable home. The early cultures of Britain and Ireland gave little heed to such harsh asceticism, instead finding holiness in the everyday ~ indeed, finding sanctity through the pleasures of the senses, rather than denigrating them.

As already suggested in the previous chapter, poetry can be many things ~ a consuming spiritual vision; witty banter; humorous nonsense; or emotional catharsis. It is this latter category that is alluded to when talking of the healing power of poetry. For the poet to pour their heart out in a song of mourning, lost love, despair etc. can be a profound release. Though, equally, one may suggest that being on the receiving end of a love poem can itself be wonderfully uplifting for the reader/listener. I speak theoretically here... no one has ever written me a love poem, and I doubt they ever will now (boohoo, sob, sob!) In my next incarnation I hope to be pretty enough to receive such things.

Early Irish stories have numerous references to the three strains of music: *goltraí* (the weeping enchantment), *gentraí* (the laughing enchantment), and *suantraí* (the sleeping enchantment). These musical styles were personified as the three sons of the goddess Boann and Uaithne, the harpist in the service of the Dagda (sometimes the name is also given to the magical harp itself, which was also called Daurdabla and Coir Cethair Chuir). Boannd was the wife of the Dagda, who in his turn is usually described as the father of Brigit.

The first of these Noble Strains, *goltraí*, may be conceived of as a cathartic healing magic that releases pent up emotion in the audience, be that grief, rage, unrequited love, or whatsoever else.

The second of these Noble Strains, *gentraí*, may have been humorous or bawdy verse set to music. Laughter, we are so often told, is the best medicine (though if you have an embarrassing rash, it's worth still applying the ointments).

The third of these Noble Strains, *suantraí*, may have essentially been lullabies or even trance-inducing tunes. As someone who has suffered regular bouts of insomnia for many years now, I can testify to the psychological harm it causes and the rejuvenating qualities of a good night's sleep. The more shamanically inclined may see *suantrai* as a means to enter ecstatic states, receive visions, or travel to astral dimensions.

In earlier times February would not have been a pleasant month, fully into winter ~ either freezing hard ground, or freezing mud-drenched soil; either way, not much fun for travelling to meet up with friends and relatives. The other three big festivals were marked with large fairs and gatherings, but not Imbolc. Rather, this festival was a quiet family occasion, one celebrated by those within a household and maybe their immediate neighbours. It is a time to sit by the hearth fire and loose yourself in the dancing flames, to think of the cold, harsh world outside and how fortunate you are to be (hopefully) well-fed, well-watered, well-loved and warm.

Well into medieval times the feasts marking the start of winter was marked with the giving of food to the poor, who often assumed the guise of the dead. The Welsh feast of *Calan Gaeaf* (equivalent to the Gaelic Samhain) encouraged the poor of each parish to "disguise" themselves with soot on their faces and legally[6] beg for food under the pretence that they were the *Cenhadon y Meirw*, the Company of the Dead.

The coldness of February is harsh for many small animals, and an ideal time to feed them ~ a sort of furred and feathered version of the *Cenhadon y Meirw*. Many Pagans (and others) leave out offerings of milk at Imbolc, probably lapped up by the neighbourhood moggies ~ hopefully not the hedgehogs, for whom cow's milk can be quite unhealthy. In reflecting on our own fortunate comforts, it becomes an appropriate time to stretch out a helping hand to those less blessed; either through impersonal donations to charities, or by actually giving food directly to hungry wild animals, or hungry humans (or, in the latter case, perhaps extending an invite for more general warmth and companionship to someone you know to be down on their luck).

Many elderly people may have enough to eat and drink, but can so often be socially isolated and deeply lonely as all the people they once knew die off. The hearth fire is not just a source of heat and a means to cook the stew, but also the focus of friendship, family and love.

Sisters of the Hearth - This first piece is a celebration of the three sisters collectively known as Brigit, whom most linguists and many historians hold to be the identical to the Romano-British deity Brigantia. One sister is the goddess of the blacksmith's forge, the other of the healing flames, and the third of poetic inspiration. The concept of sisterhood (or any other familial relationship) amongst the divine is best understood as symbolic, a human approximation of the relationships that exist between entities whose existences are really quite alien to anything we experience.

The metre is the same simplified variation on the *rannaigheacht mór* as previously used in the Sky Tribe poem.

Sisters of the Hearth

I am the smith's fierce forge-fire;
Leaden lumps to fine-honed tools
Transfigured, crucible pyre
Sloughs off the dross, my heat schools.

I am the healer's passion,
Stiff bodies eased, sore wounds seared,
Rekindling minds left ashen,
Pains soothed, life no longer feared.

I am the poet's flame-tongue,
Words licked white hot, phrases fused,
Lyrics wrought; mind's anvil sung,
Verbal sculptures burnished, hued.

Red-gold dancing, weaving force,
Feeds the medic's urge to heal,
Guides the wright upon his course,
As hot praise from bards shall reel.

I am the hearth-fire burning,
Whose beacon-blaze on cold night
Stirs tired wanderer's yearning;
Warms aching bones, cures heart's blight.

Goddess am I, formed from pride
In the land, in kith and kin,
Host Law by which all abide:
To repay our love all try.

Bona na Croin - February is known as the wolf month in Gaelic (and, indeed, on the Anglo-Saxon calendar as recorded by Bede). Wolves are an obsession of mine, and so a lupine poem just had to be written! Fionn was the warrior-druid who led the Fianna war bands, somewhat like the Merrie Men of Anglo-Saxon folklore, in that they dwelt in the wild and lived outside the regular bounds of law. In later times such bands of men (and the occasional woman) were called *diberga*, and are described as going a-wolfing in much the same way as bands of bolshy Norsemen went a-Viking. *Bona na croin* is an old Gaelic saying that translates as, neither collar nor crown (in other words being subservient to none, neither king nor Church).

This is a version of the *deibide guilbnech* metre.

Bona na Croin

Neither your collar nor crown
Shall I wear ~ my nose not brown,
Nor I some clown in your court,

In chains brought ~ a wolf to town.

By no oath bound to your King,
To my Gods alone I sing,
Grey shadow hiding from sight
To keep the rite from waning.

In red gold you dress these slaves,
What throne can forget Nine Waves?
In deep caves our flame I shield,
Never to yield to such knaves.

Collars serve to reign dogs in,
Quell their nerve with shades and sin.
Wild wolfs kin such bangles scorn,
Free-born I stay, son of Fionn.

My brothers hunted, slain, skinned.
Yet still my cries ride the wind,
Numbers thinned, but still we wait,
For your hate, we have not sinned.

Now the lone hunters take heed,
Upon the Great Stag we feed,
Blood for mead. His death our life,
Ends this strife, stirs this dried seed.

The old packs come together,
Ties that fear cannot sever,
Endeavour in pride to stand
In the Wolf Land, forever.

Brigit's Song - Back to Brigit again! As well as governing over the fires of poetry, smithing and healing, she is also a goddess of the hearth fire that burns at the centre of the home ~ literally so in the days when people lived in roundhouses with fire pits in the middle. As such she embodies the virtue of hospitality, so important to the Iron Age cultures of Britain, Ireland and numerous other places too.

The concept of *dán* referred to in the last verse is a fascinating one, worth expanding upon. The word has two primary meanings that, according to a Gaelic linguist of my acquaintance (I have no pretensions to being able to do more than grunt my way through a dozen or so words of Irish) originate from different roots. Whilst there may be no philological link, the two interpretations dovetail beautifully. *Dán* can mean either a talent or skill (especially a poetic one, and indeed describes a particular poetic metre), and also fate or destiny. Many early cultures believed in the presence of a cosmic force that shaped all, or at least a part, of what befalls us in life. The Egyptians spoke of *ma'at*, the eternal balance or proper order of things, whilst the Germanic and Scandinavian tribes talked in terms of *wyrd* and *orlog*.

To my mind, *dán* is the cosmic force giving us each gifts ~ skills, talents, abilities, maybe problems and challenges that turn out to have silver linings ~ and requiring of us that we follow the old adage of a gift begetting a gift. We are given talent for chemistry, or singing, or baking fruitcake (always a valuable skill) and must in our turn use it, not just to improve our own lives, but also to better the world around us.

Brigit's Song ~

Hearth-warmed war hounds relish rest,
With zest sing the tales of yore.
Mead-mulled lore keepers love best
To guest at Her hall once more.

Deep-hearted maid of high mien,
Poets reign by Her sweet aid,
Names fade not, but glory gain,
No vain deed, but honour made.

Frail snowdrops bloom in Her wake,
Hearts ache for the spring to flow,
Shoots grow. Emerges the snake,
Yearnings slake whilst life moves slow.

Frost-fell nights call us to clan,
Bride can lead us from dark plights,
Set our sights to summer's plan,
Weaving dán around our hearth.

Three Flames - A short piece this, again looking at the triple nature of Brigantia and the interweaving of her aspects. Each verse deals with one of the sisters. The repetitive elements of the verses remind me of Egyptian poetry, which also involves repeated invocations and praises. Little is known of Egyptian poetry (partly due to the problems in reconstructing the language), and so this is a form that I am still trying to get my head round. There is no specific story about the origins of Egyptian poetry, but language in general was considered the gift of ibis-headed Tehuti and his sometime consort Seshet, guardian of libraries.

The metre is a much-simplified version of the *seadna*, without the complex use of alliteration (which was beyond my tiny mind, on this particular occasion).

Three Flames

Light of compassion white burning,
Thaw the ice that scalds my mind

Stir the flesh from torpor afresh,
Night-blind, scars mesh; pray be kind.

Light of invention fierce burning:
Wit our tool, the world to style,
Hammers blade or share, cost displayed
By use, while trade shows our guile.

Light of creation lust burning
Gifts wise wren-wings to my word
That trumps king's cunning through kenning,
Spurred bards penning ~ tales conjured.

The Sacred Pine - The following, somewhat stroppy poem was written in reaction to reading the story of a Gaulish saint, Martin of Tours, who was in the habit of hacking down sacred trees. One victim of his axe was a pine tree much beloved by the Pagans of ancient France. I could find no indication as to the time of year when the old fool played lumberjack, so the comparison of pine resin to snow is a dose of poetic licence. The metre is a Welsh one, the *englyn cyrch*.

The Sacred Pine

Martin, sainted, midst the Gaul
Wandered preaching, screeching fool.
Churches built in foreign fields
Reaped rich yields, a papal haul.

Martin, sainted, cut his cloak
Swathed the naked, coinless folk;
Done robbing took to robbing
Forest king whose branches spoke.

Martin, sainted, roused his flock,
Ancient ways to hate and mock.
Temple wrecked by zealous sons,
The Shining Ones call to block.

Martin, sainted, seized a blade,
Stormed the sun god's holy glade,
There to hack the mighty pine,
Tree divine, whence Druids prayed.

Martin, sainted, saw the rage
Sparked within the forest sage,
Dropped the hatchet, turned and fled:
Pine bled, cleansing sap saint's wage.

Martin, sainted, failed to cleave
The hallowed tree, where sprites weave
And pagans sacrifice make;
Branches shake ~ but do not grieve.

Pine tree, sacred, held its land;
Temples built by mortal hand
Were lost, but our roots go deep,
Old ways keep, the ages spanned.

Resin weeps white amidst the snow,
Fragrant frost in solstice glow.
Old Gods rejoice; evergreen
Light in meanest hour we show.

Anam Chara – this poem celebrates the almost certainly Christian tradition within early Ireland of the 'soul friend' (not to be confused with the romantic notion of a soul mate). It refers to a spiritual mentor or counsellor, providing solace and strength to the soul. In some respects the *anamchara* foreshadowed the role of the Father Confessor, though it would appear that the role could be held by anyone (not just an ordained priest) and even by women. It is possible that some similar institution of spiritual mentoring existed amongst the tribes in Pagan times, though there is no written evidence of it.

The poem is in the *Deibhidhe* metre, and was written for a ceremony focussed on friendships important to those taking part. To smoor, incidentally, means to bank up a fire to keep its embers warm overnight so as to be easily relit come the next day.

Anam Chara

Friend of my soul, loyal hound,
What was love till you I found?
King's gold fades within your fold
As we grow old ~ wealth untold.

With wood-wise words tend the flame
That Brighid kindled and gave name.
Ghost smoke trails a fragrant cloak,
Old ways invoke for clan folk.

Your laughter plays the joy-strain,
Harp-strings pluck, charm away pain.
Tale-smith jests with jaded pith
Lifting hearts with kin and kith.

Hopes, hates, loves, and dreams he keeps,
Oath-bound in silence he weeps.
My shield from life's battlefield,
My comrade's guild grants no yield.

Faces fall like autumn leaves,

Through the web memory weaves.
Names forgotten, more and more.
Yet you stay sure, my heart smoor.

Praise my name with verses proud,
Your lips call me from the shroud.
In grave-songs my cold corpse bathe,
Such sweet words swathe, my Soul Friend.

[6] For the rest of the year begging was illegal. Parish councils and churches often kept funds for the desperately poor, but these were usually quite limited and those dependent on such hand-outs were often resented

Chapter Three

Beltaine

The season of summer marked the return of the warrior bands to the woods and mountains, leaving their families to farm in peace. Poetry can have a militant aspect to it. A large swathe of medieval Welsh and Irish poetry was devoted to recording battles, and boosting the military reputations of assorted kings and warlords.

It was at Beltaine that the divine Tuatha Dé Danann arrived in Ireland, in one account descending in a great swathe of cloud upon the Iron Mountain in modern County Leitrim. When the mists cleared, the Gods were revealed in all their glory. Beltaine has strong themes of land claiming. In the context of poetry, this brings to mind the Metrical Dindshenchas, a large body of poetry recording the stories and tales of the sacred land ~ why certain hills were odd shapes; how particular lakes sprang into being; why a bridge is called what it's called etc. The Dindshenchas relates the myths of the Irish landscape, but it is my belief (or hope) that Britain would once have had its own comparable body of stories ~ perhaps stories captured in poetry and song.

As well as celebrating victory (or commiserating defeat) an interesting form of aggressive poetry can be seen in the *áer*, a form of legally sanctioned satire in prose or poetic form used to pillory those who refused to conform to law or social standards. Alongside the legal means, the law of early Ireland also acknowledged the existence of illegal, undeserved satires that could be used almost as a form of blackmail. The Brehon law codes specified a number of illegal uses of satire, including:

- Mocking a person's appearance;
- Making known an otherwise private physical blemish;

- Coining a derogatory nickname that sticks;
- Repeating a satire composed by another poet.

One example of a dangerous poetic *áer* is the *glám dícind* (a prose *áer* being called an *aisnés*). Myth portrays the *glám dícind* as a potent curse, capable of maiming or killing a victim. This was more than just a rude or sarcastic ditty; it was a potent weapon. How the average "Irishman in the street" saw this form of poetry is a separate issue. Whilst storytellers saw it as deadly, average people may or may not have been suitably afraid of its power.

The Book of Ballymote contains a tract, *'Cis lir fodla aire?'*, which describes ten types of legally permissible satire:

- *mac bronn*; son of womb / son of sorrow. A lampoon told only to one person;
- *dallbach*; blindness / innuendo. A satire against an anonymous target, with three subtypes –
  - "Firmly established"; where the scurrilous accusations can be easily proven;
  - "Lightly established"; where the allegations are harder to prove;
  - "Not established"; mere gossip;
- *focal i frithshuidiu*; word in opposition. Written as a quatrain of praise but with a hint of sarcasm.
- *tár n-aíre*; outrage of satire. A poem which makes unflattering comparisons between the target and something unfortunate;
- *tamall aíre*; touch of satire. A toned down version of an *tár n-aíre*;
- *tár molta*; outrage of praise. A ludicrously over-the-top praise poem that lauds virtues which the target patently lacks;
- *tamall molta*; touch of praise. Damning with faint praise;
- *lánaír*; full satire. Naming and shaming in gory detail;

- *ainmedh*; basic sarcasm;
- *glám dícind*; a magical satire.

This last style of magical poem is quite intriguing. It is described in the *Uraicecht na Riar,* a book of Irish laws. The spell could not be officially cast until a body of 30 laymen, 30 bishops and 30 poets had convened ~ emphasising that this was a heavy duty social sanction, and not just a fit of literary pique on the part of the poet. It is assumed that in pre-Christian times Druids would have taken the role of the bishops. If the august body decided that a *glám dícind* was warranted, the target would be first subject to a *troscad* or legal hunger strike. If the person still refused to relent on whatever matter had caused offence, then an *Ollamh*[7] and six lesser poets, one of each of the poetic grades. At dawn, when the wind blew from the north, the poets would climb a hill at the boundary of seven lands, where a hawthorn tree[8]. Each of the seven *filidh* stood around the tree, and held a sling-stone and a thorn from the tree. Each poet recited a verse of the curse before putting the stones and thorns at the root of the thorn.

One wonders that anyone ever bothered trying to lay such a cumbersome curse, and possibly discouragement lay at the very root of its complexity.

The irate poet Cairbre, who had been shoddily treated by the monarch, used the first recorded *glam* against Bres, the vain king of the Tuatha Dé Danann.

The form used by Cairbre made no mention of committees, hawthorn trees, or any of the other procedures and so was perhaps a more simplified form of magic. The curse visited Bres' own sins upon him. Whitley Stokes translated the satire as follows:

Without food quickly on a dish:
Without a cow's milk whereon a calf grows;
Without a man's abode in the gloom of night:

Without paying a company of story-tellers, let that be Bres'
   condition,
Let there be no increase in Bres.

In his book on early Irish law codes, Fergus Kelly noted that at least certain satirical poems had to be accompanied by the poet adopting a specific physical posture, called the *córrguinech* or crane posture. This awkward and somewhat yoga-like stance involved standing on one leg, pointing with one hand and keeping one eye closed. Whether all satirical poems had to be delivered in this manner or not, is uncertain.

Why cranes should have been considered dangerous, potentially even malicious, is uncertain. There are a number of one-eyed characters in Irish myth, and they are usually hostile figures. The wintry Cailleach is often referred to as missing an eye, and Goll mac Morna was responsible for the death of Fionn's father ~ though he later came on side and loyally served the boy he had orphaned. The most infamous figure is, technically, not actually a Cyclops. The gigantic Balor lead the hordes of deadly *Fomóiri* ogres who emerged from the oceans to lay waste to Ireland. He did actually have two eyes, though one was of huge proportions and could emit a sort of death-ray that splattered his enemies.

In a desert country the monocular image could be seen as emblematic of the harsh sun, though this scarcely applies to temperate Ireland. However, many of the early Church Fathers came from parched lands and brought their fascination for harsh and abstemious living with them (hence the number of places in Ireland incorporating the loan-word *disert*, such as *Disert Mhartain*). It is possible that the prevalence of the burning eye may be more to do with Christian thought than Druidic myth.

The Druid's Vision – A departure from the strict metrical forms so far used, this bizarre tripe is the closest I have come to overt satire. It was written largely to help fill a space in a magazine (Pagan Dawn) that a good friend, Arlea Anschütz, was editing back in 2007. It loosely qualifies as Celtic, in as much as it is a parody[9] of the seminal works of William Topaz McGonagall the rather unlamented poet of my university town of Dundee.

The Druid's Vision

'Twas in the year two-thousand-nought-and-seven
That I went on up to yon Druidic heaven
(Though when I say up, it could have been down
Or sideways, so hard to tell when enfolded in the Goddess's
    gown).
At the OdbOd ritual to honour Eostre,
Our souls through a Vision Quest we strove to foster.
Away to the Otherworld I soon went,
As to the bard over his bodhran bent,
And there came to me an ancestral ghost
For amongst those gathered, I was favoured the most.
Tartan-swathed came the long-bearded divine,
Green and sparkly, I saw his aura shine.
"Who are you?", the ancient voice did croak,
"A Druid from the modern world", in whispers I spoke.
"A Druid?" those bushy eyebrows rose, "Which tribe do ye
    serve?"
"No tribe, for I am a Hedge Druid" said I with verve.
"A what?" queried the venerable sage,
So I explained ~ perhaps he had forgotten, being of such
    advanced age?
"Oh Taranis!" his head it shook sadly.
"Who?" I asked ~ he glared at me madly.
"What in the name of the Gods are ye doing here?"

"A druid ritual to the Maiden Goddess Eostre." Said I, his
　　mood turned queer
Asked he next if I knew my elbow from my arse,
(Clearly a Zen test that I was eager to pass)
I reeled off my OdbOd bardic grades ~ composed as a poem,
　　in blank verse
Unimpressed he seemed, indeed his mood grew far worse.
"Are there nay Druids true in the age whence you dwell?"
So I told him of Supreme Arch Druid Tarquin Fortesque,
　　who's just swell,
Who wrote a book, and is carried to conference on a
　　decorated bier
(Though there are no personality cults here),
An ancient Druid blessing then of the mystic did I beg,
Laid upon me his staff ~ the bruise is now faded to the size of
　　a goose egg ~
Then did the tree priest begin to fade, but his last words I
　　caught,
A blessing on the breeze: *"Imeacht gan teacht ort"*,
Though I am a Celt in heart, I do not speak the lingo,
But know that I am truly blessed ~ praise the Goddess, by
　　Jingo!

The Honey–Tongued - The following poem was written in praise
of Ogma, or Ogmios as we more often tend to refer to him. In
medieval Wales bards were sometimes referred to as carpenters
of song ~ perhaps drawing on the close association between
knowledge and trees. It's an image that I decided to run with in
this poem! Inis Toraigh is an island of the coast of Ireland that
was believed to be the home of the monstrous *Fomóiri* who
plagued so many of the races that tried to inhabit Eire. One of
Ogma's titles is *Cermait*, which translates as Honey Mouthed. In
our 21st century British idiom we would be more inclined to
describe someone as honey-tongued, hence the title of the poem.

The Honey-Tongued

Ogma, carpenter of song,
Harvest the forest of thought,
Carve the timbre of my voice,
That the nemeton be wrought.

Gnarled the Tree whence language born,
Old the God whom Ogam made.
Youthful yet the lips that speak
And the hand that wields the blade.

Orna praises the hero,
Makes memory history.
In Ogma's service he works,
Freed from dark Inis Toraigh.

Honey-tongue, caress my ears.
Amber tales in rivers run
Through the stream-beds of my heart,
Savoured by my loved one.

In the wildwoods of the mind,
Strange beasts rut, conceive new words
That sing in branches high above,
At the festival of birds.

Radiant-faced Ogma hears
The melding of words to verse.
Stories told, a joy to him
Who acts as Memory's nurse.

Before the Owl Takes Flight - This poem, in the Welsh *Byr a Thoddaid* metre, was written to celebrate Blodeuwedd, the flower maiden from Welsh mythology who was conjured forth from a cauldron of blossoms. She was destined to marry Lleu, though the relationship was not a happy one. Cursed by Gwydion for her apparent betrayal of his nephew with another man, she was turned into an owl and never again able to enjoy the gentle sun.

This piece has previously been included in the souvenir programme, along with works by all the other entrants, for the 2008 Flag Fen Eisteddfod (what I won... just thought I'd throw that bit of cheesy bragging in here).

Before the Owl takes Flight

Let your sap rise up in greeting
Of the tender light so fleeting,
Bright the blossoms of the broom, sweep fresh joy,
Golden boy, future groom.

Old Math's words the earth does waken,
Flowers from their slumber shaken,
Winter's brittle tomb cracks with painful sigh,
Butterfly starts her reign.

Time does youth its bright colours fleece,
From the Gods we our rainbow lease,
Unfurl your petals whilst the sky can see
Such beauty ~ be not shy.

Decaying winter exorcise
With rich perfumes and lover's sighs,
Nodding heads of flowers beat life's rhythm
With them languid bees meet.

Honeyed love blooms beneath the sun,
Yet wilts without its chosen one.
Growing free she is savoured best of all,
What fool plucks her in jest?

When the light is gone, what remains?
Bloodless spectral white, shadow stains
The bower through which the ghostly owl sails,
Wails in the night, pale host.

Cavort with her whilst she is here,
Treasure blossoms like jewels dear,
When all is grey and the white owl swoops low,
Know that the dawn brings light.

The Herb Wife - This poem is in *Rannaigheacht Mor* metre and
was written for an open ritual held in a Suffolk woods to honour
Airmid, the goddess of herbalism and daughter of the god of
surgery. In the tale her brother Miach was killed by their father
who was outraged at his audacity in trying to outdo the medical
achievements of his elders. Even after his burial Miach continued
to defy his father, by growing healing herbs from his own grave,
which Airmid then gathered and used.

The Herb Wife

My cloak on the ground I'll lay,
Father's harsh words unheeding,
Upon it wise herbs display,
Scant pay for brother bleeding.

Bright Miach dead, gone from me,
Our father's rage is sated,
From death knowledge does not flee,

Brotherly wisdom waited.

"To cure is fine," Diancecht said
"But death must remain the end,
Lest the land it go unfed.
Man's thread to cut I intend."

"Father fair," my sibling sued
"Death is but an ill to cure,
Eternity may be wooed,
Flesh imbued to e'er endure."

"Never so!" Roared our stern sire,
"Cut flesh shall wither, worms feed,
What is lost, consign to fire,
Reach no higher than hubris, heed!"

Young stags their own glory chase,
Vision's flame it does consume,
Old stags thinking to save face,
Do base deeds that gather gloom.

An arm that should be bare bone,
A crown that should be passed on.
On Miach's grave sits a stone,
Costly throne. Gain to dark Donn.

Through death brother's Will shall out,
Flesh was his concern and mine,
Healing herbs from decay sprout,
Donn's law flout, his sacred shrine.

On woven form plants I lay
Lungwort, heartsease, knitbone root,

One cunning herb for each day,
May I the herbwife's trade ply.

Taliesin's Tale - This rather long poem is written in the simplest of the Welsh metres, the *englyn milwr* or Soldier's Metre. The story of Taliesin always goes down well with a young audience, and is also one of the stories that I get the most requests for from adults ~ so it seemed only fair to try and encapsulate the myth in poetic guise (even if it does verge on doggerel at times).

Taliesin's Tale

Morvran's mother, grieving womb
Spawned grim fiend fit for the tomb,
Hidden in the deepest gloom.

Daughter like the dawn cool bright,
Shields her brother with starlight,
Shadows grant but brief respite.

Croaking cormorant weeps rage,
Trapped within his fleshly cage.
No king he, but perhaps sage?

Upon the hearth the cauldron set,
Hope and wrath by moonlight met,
Magic wrought to meet the debt.

Tower empty, servants fled,
From bard's hall, the music bled,
The Cauldron fires go unfed.

Morda blind, his faith still true,
Untouched he by that vile hue,

Scorns not infant Afaggdhu.

One old man to feed the flame,
Sad silent this hall of fame,
Help now sought to lift the shame.

The moon she calls far and near,
Gwion answers, knows no fear,
Stewards the hall once so dear.

Twelve tides turn on her quest
For Awen herbs rare and best,
For her son she takes no rest.

Gwion stirs and Morda tends,
Till at last the hour descends,
Then the mighty Cauldron rends.

Sweet Awen drops fly out Three
Past the raven from the sea,
On to Gwion, wisest he!

Knowledge floods within his vein,
Dark infant robbed howls with pain,
Mother turns with livid mein.

Gwion to his heels takes flight,
Seeks refuge in morning light,
Hot pursued by baying spite.

"Fleet of foot and fiery fair",
Shaped by thought, he now a hare,
Red streak flashes beyond care.

Blue skinned, sharp-fanged moon-led witch
Turns herself to howling bitch,
Snaps at hare's tail, blood so rich.

"In that deep lake I could dive!"
Change again to stay alive,
Salmon now, on weed-bed writhe.

Greyhound savage now goes meek,
Shifts shape into otter sleek,
Hunts fish still in vengeful pique.

"Shelter false, oh for the skies!",
Salmon leaps, spreads wings and flies
Far from water-dog, he sighs.

Lake-sprite jumps and too takes wing,
Hawk-eye spots sparrow's ending,
Deadly flight the forests ring.

"Were I but a tiny grain!",
Hope to deed, he hides in vain,
One amongst a thousand lain.

Hawk upon the threshing floor,
Gulps a seed, then eats some more,
Now a hen in farmer's store.

Eyeless, earless, Gwion small
Hopes for rescue, little fool,
Black death finds him in farm hall.

Chicken clucks in triumph now,
So to end her bitter vow,

Turns to home as great white sow.

Nine lamps light the darksome night,
Her womb fills to fullest might,
A child born to make all right.

Wondrous boy, sister's brother,
Morvran's hate sure to smother,
Set afloat, tearful mother.

On the tides baby carried,
Till in salmon weir harried,
Found by prince, whilst he tarried.

Elphin looks into the bag,
"Radiant brow!" says the wag,
Taliesin named, son of the hag.

Summer's Sisters - The following slightly Catholic ditty, in *Rannaigheacht ghairid* metre, was written for a Beltane festival. The festival is traditionally associated with the blossoming of the hawthorn tree. The blackthorn blooms earlier in the season, and is much associated with gruesome magic (possibly due to the number of infections carried on its thorns). The allusion to the Summer Queen is in part inspired by folk practices on the Isle of Man where a person dressed up as the Summer Queen does battle with the Winter Queen.

Summer's Sisters

Sisters we,
Sibyls of sweet summer's spree
Roll the verdant carpet out
Leaves sprout, buds stir, sap flows free.

Blackthorn mourns
At winter's grave, weeps harsh thorns,
White mantilla fluttering fair
Falls where broken hart shed horns.

Whitethorn shields
The Summer Queen, may staff wields.
Musk-rich maid, the she-wolf howls,
Domain prowls, skirting rich fields.

Sisters they,
Dark and light eternal play
One to grieve and one to grow,
Savour sloe this Beltane day.

Cu Chulainn at the Ford – To finish this chapter, a warriors'
poem recording the emotional crux of the *Táin Bo Cúailnge*, the
great saga of Irish myth. In this excerpt from the tale the great
hero of Connaught, Ferdiad, was tricked into battling his blood
brother and friend beneath the blanket (a possible allusion to a
male lover), Cu Chulainn of Ulster. The Ulsterman wins, but
instantly regrets the death of his dearest friend. *Tech Duinn* is the
name of a small island off the Irish coast, which was regarded as
either the home of the dead or at least a stopping post on their
journey to the Afterlife This poem is in *Ae Freisilighe* metre.

Cu Chulainn at the Ford

On Scathach's isle befriended,
Our sky bright then, no stormcloud,
With Ferdiad, beloved,
Under blanket, not deathshroud.

Quickly you flew resentful.

Did you think me so shallow?
Were Medb's wiles so successful?
Friendship left too long fallow.

The Ford, bitter memory,
Where love and hate so muddied.
Lots cast, we faced warily,
Truth lost, broken and bloodied.

Red stream and red victory,
Friendship for honour traded,
A boast made so hollowly,
Over times past we waded.

Now only spear penetrates,
Sunders both hearts, left lifeless,
My name this deed denigrates
Laeg's praise falls on me, worthless.

You blushed once, so wonderful,
Now blanched, bereft of passion.
Forgive your Hound, remorseful,
Think well of me in Tech Duinn.

[7] An ollamh is the highest rank of poet, and the modern Irish word for a professor.

[8] A convoluted requirement, but trees have often been used as boundary markers and it may even be that hawthorns were the tree of choice for planting at land boundaries.

[9] Can one pastiche a person who is virtually a walking caricature anyway?

Chapter Four

Lughnasadh

As previously mentioned, one of the functions of the bards and *filidh* was the memorising and recitation of genealogies. Poetry can be an ideal way of celebrating history, but also a way of giving thanks to those ancestors duly remembered. Numerous cultures both ancient and modern place great emphasis on using memory as a prime way of giving honour to the revered dead. This may take the form of tending the graves of loved ones, eating special meals at the graveside, decorating altars with photos, reciting their names and deeds etc.

A recitation may, of course, be a simple prose roll call of the dead, or a slightly expanded version in which some deeds and qualities are mentioned. A poetic recollection of the dead has two added benefits: firstly, it is easier to remember a rhyming list than a prose one; and secondly, it requires more mental effort (which adds to the sacrificial value) to compose.

The feast of Lughnasadh, though named after a male deity (Lugh) was traditionally said to be a funereal commemoration of a goddess, Tailtiu. Those forms of Paganism inspired mostly by Wicca tend to see the early August festival as having a masculine feel ~ talking most often of the death of the Corn King, John Barleycorn and other male figures. The Irish tradition celebrated the death of a feminine presence, who had keeled over with exhaustion after turning the previously untameable wilderness of Connaught (where her people, the Fir Bolg, dwelt) into agricultural land.

Within our ritual group, Lughnasadh is a time for reflecting on the sacrifices made by the women in our lives, and in the world in general. Relatively few British women die in childbirth these days, but it is still a high-risk in many parts of the world as it once was in this land.

Professor Liam Breatnach translated an obscure and untitled poem appearing in the *Auraicept na n-Eces*, a book for grammarians and scholars some parts of which date back as far as the 7th century. Excerpts from his translation are quoted below. The original work is attributed to a monk called Néde mac Adne, who placed his words in the mouth of Amergin White-knee, and it is written in a Christian context with references to the monotheist deity (though many modern Pagans take it as an example of druidic mysticism). Professor Breatnach has suggested *"In Coire Érmae"* as a suitable title for the poem, whilst others favour the title suggested by Annie Power, The Cauldron of Poesy.

Historians and medievalists tend not to place much emphasis on this text, regarding it as fairly minor. However, many modern Pagans tend to view it as a precious remainder from polytheist times. I am yet to be convinced of this view, but include mention of it simply because the contemporary perspective is worth considering in any work on Insular Celtic poetry.

It begins, *"Mine is a fine cauldron of dutiful maintenance / Which God has given me out of the mysterious elements"*. In Gaelic poetry these elements, or *duile*, tend not to be the four made popular by the Greeks, but rather sets of seven or nine aspects of the natural world such as rock, sun, moon, storm etc.

The poem discusses three mystical cauldrons which exist within the poet, and that can be turned by various means. Some authors, such as Erynn Rowan Laurie, tend to see a parallel between the three cauldrons and the seven-chakra energy centres of Vedic tradition. It seems to me that, if the Insular Celts did indeed hold to some sort of chakric-style belief, then one might expect more evidence of it to survive than one obscure allusion in a densely cryptic poem. In its heyday the religion of the Druids and their fellow tribesmen was probably as involved and sophisticated as any other faith. However, so little of it has survived to the 21st century that there are infuriating gaps. Trying to get a sense of what they religion taught is like trying to reassemble a 1000-piece jigsaw without any picture as a guideline and 950 of the pieces missing. It is extremely tempting to turn to other religions, especially ones from that same historical period, to fill in the gaps. This is not necessarily a bad thing, but sometimes it can be too easy to envision a full heat wave on the basis of one passing swallow.

At risk of digressing (me... lose the thread, or even the plot, say it ain't so, Joe) an example of myth grafting can be found in the search for a Celtic creation myth. Whilst the *Lebor Gabála Érinn* gives an account of the creation of Ireland itself, there is no complete creation-of-the-world story within Welsh or Irish myth cycles. There are scraps and possibilities, but nothing cohesive. Many cultures have a common motif involving a dismembered giant. The Chinese have the tale of Pangu, the Norse their myth of Ymir, and the Hindus have the tale of Purusha ~ in each case a giant exists back in an early pre-time, before being chopped up and the world created from the various body parts. Some historians have speculated that there may once have been a disembowelled Celtic giant, though no overt story survives (or, if it does, moulders untranslated in some university basement). Evidence for this claim is drawn from a tenuous account in a 13th century manuscript (Additional MS 4783, folio 7a) about Adam:

"It is worth knowing what Adam was made of, that is, of seven parts: the first part, of earth; the second part, of sea; the third part, of sun; the fourth part, of clouds; the fifth part, of wind; the sixth part, of stones; the seventh part, of the Holy Ghost.

The part of the earth, this is the man's body; the part of the sea, this is the man's blood; the part of the sun, his face and his countenance; the part of the clouds, his thoughts; the part of the wind, his breath;

the part of the stones, his bones; the part of the Holy Ghost, his soul."

Admirers of Cathal O' Searcaigh may see strong echoes to his love poetry, in which the body of the beloved fuses with the features of the sacred landscape. It is by no means an exclusively Celtic approach, but is fully in keeping with the culture that saw a goddess' breasts in two hills, and a river born of another goddess being caught short and needing a piddle!

How widespread or ancient this particular concept, of a heptadic division to human nature, is uncertain. It may emulate the seven hierarchies within the Irish Church, or be based upon the seven bodies of medieval astrology, or something far older. The Ancient Egyptians believed humanity to have a nine-fold nature, so there is certainly plenty of historical mileage to be had in a poly-psychic concept.

To amble back to the point, if ever there was one, there may once have been a myth told of some archaic giant or monster whose blood became the seas, bones the mountains and so forth. Maybe. If such a tale did once exist, I suspect that different tribes would have given that primal creature different names, rather than there being one neatly ordered tale common to all the tribal nations.

One of the central concepts within these giant myths is that all things are connected, related, fundamentally of the same substance. That seems to me an idea quite in keeping with what little we know of Druidic doctrine, though that is of no guarantee that such a story definitely existed. It may be mostly wishful thinking on the part of modern commentators who (like me) cannot abide a half-finished picture.

A further aside, the account of Adam's parts is followed up by diagnostic guidelines paralleling the more widespread Greek notion of the Four Humours in which of excess or lack of a certain humour creates a particular personality type. The monk recording Adam's nature gave what basically amounts to Seven Humours or personality characteristics born of elemental imbalance.

Anyway, back to the three cauldrons ~ the Cauldrons of *Goiriath* (Warming or Incubation), *Érmae* (Motion or Vocation) and *Sois* (Knowledge or Wisdom). These cauldrons are described as being variously tipped, upside down or properly righted, which has been seized upon by those enamoured of the chakric theory ~ given that the image of moving cauldrons has some resonance with the spinning wheels of the Vedic chakras. The position of the cauldrons varies from one person to another, with the inverted position being associated with ignorance (presumably because the contents have spilled out); the tilted position with moderate skill (again because, presumably, some of the contents remain within); and, finally, the upright position with the greatest skill.

Grief, the poem instructs, can tilt the cauldron of a sage, suggesting that maybe sorrow can cause even a wise person to lose their head. Happiness can cause a gain in knowledge or wisdom, by turning that cauldron which starts upside-down and empty in everyone. On a positive note, the poem marks two forms of joy that may bring this gain in understanding:

"There are, then, two divisions of joy
through which it is converted into the Cauldron of Knowledge,
i.e. divine
joy and human joy."

This could indicate a distinction between those poets inspired by the wonders of mortal life and those having mystical or spiritual revelations. Curiously (given that a theoretically celibate monk recorded the poem) sexual joy, along with good health and the satisfaction born of composing good poetry and grounding frenzies, is listed as one of the forms of pleasure that tilt the cauldron.

The Christian imagery is integrated with Pagan symbols, as the author writes about the hazelnuts of wisdom that are to be harvested from the well of Segais ~ a magical pool owned by the old water god Nechtan and tended by his wife Boand. The old wisdoms then were not to be forsaken or ignored, but integrated with the new.

As the verse below indicates, setting the cauldron in action can potentially lift the ignoble up to higher status. In a modern context this might be seen as an alchemical metaphor for polishing rough diamonds, though in the original context it is more likely to have shown a change in social status from *doer-nemed* to *nemed* (humble to sacred).

When the poet wrote:

I acclaim the
Cauldron of Érmae
with understandings of grace
with accumulations of knowledge
with strewings of imbas,
(which is) the estuary of wisdom
the uniting of scholarship,
the streams of splendour,
the exalting of the ignoble,
the mastering of language,
quick understanding,
the darkening of speech...

He described his Cauldron of Vocation, the source of his professional, artistic and spiritual calling. All these forces, of scholarship and language and grace, blended and merged in the mind of the poet-seer. The darkening of speech could be an allusion to the secret language of poets, perhaps a combination of kennings, archaic jargon and maybe even a sign language which only fellow initiates understood.

There are numerous magical cauldrons in Celtic myth, and it is worth pausing to reflect on the significance of cauldrons to the early tribes. In a purely practical sense they were cooking puts but, given the predominance of roundhouses with central fire-pits, the cauldron became a metaphor for the very heart of the homestead. A full cauldron meant survival for people who may often have experienced starvation. As with so many other cultures of that time, hospitality towards strangers was a central value and a means of enabling long distance travel. The cauldron represented that promise of hospitality.

Breatnach is of the opinion that, at least by the time the *Auraicept* was being written down, the high caste poet-seers were solidly embedded in the Christian tradition and were mostly focussed on developing the intellectual aspects of poetry. The poetic grades describe in the *Uraichect na Riar* make it clear that even these devout churchgoers were still expected to work acts of magic and divination, so they were not completely divorced from the Pagan mysticism of their predecessors. However, it is probably fair to say that the visionary states that may have been common before Patrick were largely sidelined by the time the oldest surviving copy of the *Auraicept* was written in the 12th century.

Having said that, the 1100s also provide us with the following account from Bishop Gerald of Wales, writing about his encounter with a body of Welsh mystical poets known as the *awenyddion*:

"When you consult them about some problem, they immediately go into a trance and lose control of their senses... They do not answer the question put to them in a logical way. Words stream from their mouths, incoherently and apparently meaningless and lacking any sense at all, but all the same well expressed: and if you listen carefully to what they say you will receive the solution to your

problem. When it is all over, they will recover from their trance, as if they were ordinary people waking from a heavy sleep, but you have to give them a good shake before they regain control of themselves... and when they do return to their senses they can remember nothing of what they have said in the interval... They seem to receive this gift of divination through visions that they see in their dreams. Some of them have the impression that honey or sugary milk is being smeared on their mouths; others say that a sheet of paper with words written on it is pressed against their lips..."

It is tempting to imagine this practice as a survival of some secret Pagan magic, though if we bear in mind most of the Welsh druids were despatched by the Romans over a thousand years beforehand, then it seems a tad unlikely. Many modern churches encourage worshippers to enter ecstatic states and speak in tongues, which to most hearers' sounds like the gibberish described in the quote above. The *awenyddion* may therefore have been operating within a Christian context.

The reference to a sweet taste in the poets' mouths could be an allusion, not entirely understood by Gerald himself, to consumption of some sweet tasting mind-altering substance. The aforementioned *Coire* poem contains the line, *"a noble brew in which is brewed / the basis of all knowledge"*, which may be simple poetic imagery but again echoes the widespread association between inspiration, spiritual awakening, mystical insight and transformation, and some sort of beverage or potion.

Many modern Pagans consider Lughnasadh a sort of harvest festival, a time when we consider the rewards that we have reaped as a result of our work. There are probably only a tiny number of people these days who can make a living out of poetry, but in earlier times it appears to have been quite a lucrative profession (at least for those at the top of their game). Cormac's Glossary, a dictionary of 1400 or so Gaelic words penned by a bishop in the late 800s, gives the following description of the Cauldron of Covetousness, "*Although only the size of the head of a large cingit it had nine chains coming out of it with a hole at the end of every chain. Nine artists stood around it while the company sang, with the point of his spear fixed in the hole of the chain that was next to him. Any gifts given to the artists were put into the cauldron, hence its name, the Cauldron of Covetousness. The proper content of the cauldron was a brethnasc of pure gold weighing twelve ounces.*"

The number nine appears in various mystical contexts within Insular Celtic traditions ~ for example, the breath of nine maidens warmed the cauldron of *Annwfn*, in Welsh tradition.

Re-enacting this tradition might make for an interesting charity drive at a Pagan event, with the cauldron contents being donated to some worthy cause. Though that assumes one could find nine decent modern Pagan poets and get them to turn up in one place at one time, and stay sober long enough to perform!

The Foster Mother – this praise poem to honour Tailtiu was written for a Lughnasadh ceremony. In ancient times the bond between a foster-parent and child was often regarded as deeper than the emotional ties to biological parents. In an age when so many families include a stepparent, it is worth considering the potential for good that such people have. Too many children's fairy stories have wicked stepmothers and fathers, not enough have good ones to balance the PR out.

I'm not a parent myself (except a surrogate pack leader to a Jack Russell and a husky), but the Druid Clan to which I belong currently has one member who is a stepfather ~ and a very good one at that ~ so let's have more upbeat stepparents in children's poetry and fiction.

The Foster Mother

Bright the gifts to you I bring,
Whilst scythes swing in honey haze.
Gold the praise to you I sing,
Humbling deeds in dying days.

Mother ashen, labour's theft,
Her kin bereft, bounty's cost ~
Tailtiu lost, her grave ne'er left
Sans tears, 'reft for early frost.

Wilderness gave way to plains,
Farmers gain is grey wolves loss.
Racing horses toss their manes
Where hunting lord no more reigns.

Cattle graze, crops for sun yearn,
Field-bound men the wild wood spurn,
New ways learn to feed the ground,
To Tailtiu's mound soft they turn.

Forests fallen to plough shears,
Corn ears hark to ghosts of oak,
Wild folk whom the goddess clears,
Hunger hears not what they spoke.

Honour her, Connaught's wise queen,
Who tamed the land unseen, yet
Forget not who leads the Fian,
Woodland's wean in balance right.

Tailtiu's Tale - This sort piece, written in *trëochair* metre, is intended to be read in ritual by a woman ~ speaking as Tailtiu herself. Bua is one of the wives of Lugh, often considered to be one of the names of the Cailleach, goddess of winter. Feminists might have something to say about a man putting words into a female character's mouth, but I'm far too much of a sexist old git to pay any attention.

Taitiu's Tale

Not womb-borne
But breastfed to burgeoning
Strength on my milk, now careworn

Crushed, hollowed
From helping my Fir Bolg
Kin through hard labour hallowed.

King's consort
Calloused, soft life sacrificed
To salvage my sweet Connaught.

Wild woodland
Cleared clovered paradise,
Kine and crops praise my axe-hand.

My deathbed
Desire ~ mother's funeral
Fair: all in peace and well fed.

Songs enshrine
Loving laments undying
Whilst my feast is held divine.

Come nearer
Light of the east, Lamhfada,
Forget not my love. Dearer

Than womb-borne
You are to me, Bua's man,
Strength of my heart, now outworn.

At Tara's Gate - This poem is inspired by the story of Lugh
arriving at the gates of Tara and having to prove his worthiness
to enter by listing his many and various skills. Gamal and Camal
are the two gatekeepers whose good opinion he must win to pass
on through. Even a deity cannot assume that the world will fall
at his feet without making at least some effort. Should you ever
need to get through an interview process, he is the god to call
upon!

At Tara's Gate

Shining Tara quelled by fear,
Tributes dear, their foes wealth swelled.
Council held, though scant the cheer
With tax day near, the rage welled.

From the east a golden swain
Of handsome mien, came to feast.
The gatehouse ceased bright Lugh's train,
For his gain, a test at least.

"None shall dwell without a skill",
Cants the drill, "What can you tell?"
His arts to spell begins Scàil,
By Manann's will he learned well.

"A wood smith's art is mine to yield",
Lugh revealed, a humble start.
"Luchtar, so smart, all can build",
Danann's guild gave little part.

Each in turn the young lord gave:
A sage grave, a healer stern,
For forge burn, for harp-string crave,
For battles brave, tales spun yearn.

Gamal sneered, "These skills we know!",
His brow aglow, Lugh endeared
Not afeared, by this hard show.
"I shall go," said Lugh, still cheered.

"If you boast one who knows all."
For king's hall guard leaves his post.
Royal host does Lugh then call,
To install him with gifts most.

Gobanos - We once held a ritual to honour Gobanos, god of brewery and blacksmithing. Alongside reading the poem, we brewed up a concoction in the cauldron, with each person adding gifts of fruit. Eventually this was turned into mead ready to be drunk at the following year's ceremony.

The Irish Goibniu and Welsh Govannon are medieval forms of the earlier Iron Age name of Gobanos. The degree to which their myths continue the earlier traditions of Gobanos is debatable, but I suspect that the core has remained intact.

Dáithí Ó hÓgáin wrote about the Gaelic word *meisce*, which can mean both 'drunk' and (rarely) 'in mental ferment', which he linked to poets becoming so worked up in their artistic frenzies as to overheat and become as flush-faced as drunkards.

Any home brewers reading this book would benefit from

reading around about Gobanos and his children, the *clurichaun*. They, and comparable spirits named in other cultures, watch over the wine cellars, beer cellars, and other such places associated with brewing and storing alcohol. Make sure you give the little chaps a taste of your wares, and the dread vinegar fly and exploding demijohns should never trouble you!

Gobanos

World Wanderer knows the need
Of the parched world-weary soul,
Waters the heart's arid seed
With sweetest mead from blest bowl.

Forge's fire heats cauldron deep,
Melds honey to stream's pure blood,
White-hot blades from his coal-heap
For mead weep, slake in fresh flood.

Bee-rich steam censes his shrine
As swords in the waters sleep.
Blacksmith, beersmith, makes both fine,
Fighters and thirsters dine deep.

Where weapons wound, good ale heals,
King's hall with bright laughter rings,
The Lord before whom Truth kneels
His heart unseals, sweetly sings.

Let all toast the Brew of Age,
Secret kept by clurichauns,
That restores youth to the sage,
Goibniu's wage to our great world.

Cormac mac Art - This poem celebrates the life of the greatest of the Irish kings, Cormac mac Art. Renowned for his wisdom, fairness and magical adventures in the Otherworld, he died in the middle part of the 3rd century CE, some while before the coming of the missionaries. However, there is a late dated legend in which the Church claimed that Cormac had spontaneously converted to the worship of Jehovah as a result of a vision ~ and that the Druids had conspired to hex him to death as a result, making him asphyxiate on a fish bone! In the words of the Chronicle of Clonmacnoise, he was *"Absolutely the best king that ever reigned in Ireland before himself.... wise, learned, valiant and mild, not given causelessly to be bloody as many of his ancestors were; he reigned majestically and magnificently."* Perhaps the Church couldn't bear the thought that so famed an ancestor could be anything other than Christian? Incidentally, the Medb mentioned in the poem is a Goddess and not the Connaught queen of the same name.

This work is in *rannaigheacht ghairid* metre, which proved somewhat easier to work with than initially expected (though it did lead to my using some dreadful elision to remain within the structure).

Cormac mac Art

Wolf-reared cub
Birthed amidst Connaught's poor scrub,
From humble roots came I wild,
Art's child, far from Tara's hub.

Wisdom brewed
In forest dent he wolves hewed
My soul-stone to serve Pack's need,
Till to Man's creed I was wooed.

Beardless boy
To court came I, without ploy
My Brehon's tongue judgement borne:
Sheep shorn to woad-woman's joy.

Newfound chief
To sov'reign bed from storm heath.
Goddess proud, Red-Sided Medb,
Ninth wave of kings cuts his teeth.

Tara bound,
Man to rule from sacred ground
Where Gods haunt with apple boughs,
Peaceful vows made at its sound.

In mead Truth,
Cup's continence ample proof,
For years no lie was heard here,
No fear needed to coax sooth.

Foolish act
That shattered the royal pact,
Ill day wrathful Cellach's spear
Cost Ireland dear, eyeless wracked.

High King famed
Yet now by false death-mask shamed,
Warlord choked upon fishbone!
Lies sworn by Untrue Cup, maimed.

Imply they
That salmon lore made me clay,
Druids curse for breaking oath
By breaking loaf, in Christ's pay!

Saints ill spoke,
Ancient Gods did not me choke.
In royal grave still I rest,
Poor jest that I scorned Medb's cloak.

Fintan's guise
Was not the blest fish whose lies
Lodge bitter within my craw,
Sore pay this, great Cormac cries.

Faith I kept,
For the smirch on my name wept
Till Manann's branch shook and bliss
Deep as Medb's kiss healed her Wolf.

Harvest's Tide - A rather bleak composition this one, reflecting on humanity's often exploitative relationship to the Earth. This is written in *debide guilbnech dialtach* metre. I was in a grim mood when I wrote it.

Goibniu (Gobanos) brews the Ale of Immortality that the company of gods drink at the Feast of Age, hosted by Mannanan (Mannanos). The story, what little is left of it, is reminiscent of the Norse tale of Idunna's apples that keep the gods of Asgard young and vital. One wonders if maybe they preferred their apples brewed into cider?

Harvest's Tide

Loamed flesh to iron claws yields;
Woods felled, hills sculptured to fields.
Human love oft seeks to mould
Desires what could yet be told.

Mother's milk-sap suckles maws,

Hunger unsated, though stores
Burst with dragon-hoarded feast,
Whilst thin-fleshed remain the least.

Still she gives, abundance reigns
For her fosterlings such grains
As brew the Feast of Age, smith's toast
Served by Sea Lord, beloved host.

We are the late-coming Lords,
At battle's eve, drawing swords
Boasting skills, the gate we passed
Assumed the throne, domain vast.

Ogma's deeds we have undone,
At logic's game we have won,
Ocean's terrors conquered now,
Tailtiu dead, beneath the plough.

Our reach is long, our light spreads
The wise one in caution treads
Where we blunder; fools sent blind
By our own light, lost to mind

And yet at this August tide
We may pause in lordly stride
To thank the Mother of fields,
Who the greater power wields.

Chapter Five

Here be Dragons!

Polytheists can be quite a social lot and often extend invites to attend each other's ceremonies and festivals. It always seems polite to take something (mead, whisky, a crate of crème de muirne etc) which can include some form of entertainment ~ a story or, apposite for this tome, poetry.

The first few examples were offered up at Heathen blótar (festivals in which the making of toasts is a central act). A number of poetic metres come to us from Heathen sources, especially via the Icelandic Eddas, some examples of which follow.

Heathen poetry does not usually rhyme, but relies on phonetic alliteration ~ words that begin with the same consonant sounds and so create a rhythm. Though I'm not an expert, I suspect most of these original metres were most likely sung instead of spoken.

I rather enjoy writing Heathen poetry. It's a very social religion, and has some fascinating ideas. I've only (at this time of writing) made a mental/emotional connection with two Heathen deities, but do find a great many similarities in the ideals and worldviews between Heathenry and the form of polytheist Druidry[10] that I follow.

The populist image of a Heathen is of some big fat hairy Viking who likes swigging beer and thumping people (and the men aren't considered any better). The reality is quite different; ancient Heathens were as likely to be poets as warriors, if not both at the same time. Modern Heathens are almost as frequently academics as they are bikers or members of the Real Ale Society. Poetry and academia, as so often, make good bedfellows. Whilst some Heathens subscribe to the neo-pagan tendency of writing abysmal doggerel and squawking huffily about self-expression whenever someone points out that it's bad enough to make a Vogon[11] blush, others look to the words woven by our ancestors.

In the introduction to the poem (in the previous chapter) entitled *Gobanos*, I mentioned the sacred nature of alcohol. It is one of the markedly unusual features of the ancient and modern Pagan religions, setting them apart from most of the mainstream religions of the world. This sanctity is expressed perhaps most especially in the myths of the Northern tribes of the world.

In the Finnish epic *Kalevala*, the dangerous sorceress Louhi (who strongly echoes the Russian Baba Yaga and the Gaelic goddess Cailleach) announced that she did not understand brewing ~ which was unfortunate, as she had her daughter's wedding to Ilmarinen to cater. An old man responded with a long explanation as to the origins and making of booze by the lady Osmotar, the Beer Preparer, with the help of two maidens, Kalevatar and Kapo. Between them they created magical creatures (an albino squirrel, a marten and a bee.) Each helped them experiment with ingredients. The pinecones and bear spittle were of little use, but the honey made the brew ideal. Still they fretted over the magical ale, until a bird sang to them ~

> From a treetop sings the redbreast,
> From the aspen calls the robin:
> *'Do not grieve, thy beer is worthy,*
> *Put it into oaken vessels,*
> *Into strong and willing barrels*
> *Firmly bound with hoops of copper.'*

I love the fact that the bird advising on brewing in this *Kalevala* quote is a robin! The trinity of Kalevatar, Kupo and Osmotar may well be regarded as the goddesses or wights[12] of alcohol. The honey-ale also draws the reader to Meilikki, a goddess known as 'The Honey-rich Mother of the Woods', and rather reminiscent of the Irish deer goddess Sadb. The powers of Osmotar's wondrous brew were celebrated in a *Kalevala* verse that could well be read in honour of the brewing sprites, regardless of which Pagan tradition one follows ~

> *Said to make the feeble hardy,*
> *Famed to dry the tears of women,*
> *Famed to cheer the broken-hearted,*
> *Make the aged young and supple,*
> *Make the timid brave and mighty,*
> *Make the brave men ever braver,*
> *Fill the heart with joy and gladness,*
> *Fill the mind with wisdom-sayings,*
> *Fill the tongue with ancient legends,*
> *Only makes the fool more foolish.*

This excerpt brings to my mind a rather lovely verse from the Welsh *Canu y Medd* (The Song of Mead, originally from the *Llyfr Taliesin*) translated by Thomas Love Peacock, which makes a great blessing for a mead horn.

> *The bee tastes not the sparkling draught*
> *Which mortals from his toils obtain;*
> *That sends, in festal circles quaffed,*
> *Sweet tumult through the heart and brain.*
> *The timid, while the horn they drain,*
> *Grow bold; the happy more rejoice;*
> *The mourner ceases to complain;*
> *The gifted bard exalts his voice.*

The combination of spit and honey in this story also brings to mind the Norse tale of Kvasir, whose existence accounts for the origin of poetic inspiration. The two main families of Gods (Aesir and Vanir) sealed a peace treaty by each spitting into a jar ~ an unsanitary habit, and not one recommended as the basis for any potential blótar. The contents of this jar were then used to form a magical man called Kvasir, who wandered the nine worlds spreading wisdom and understanding. Unfortunately two malicious dwarves murdered him and poured his blood into a cauldron and two vats, mixed it with honey and made it into the most wondrous mead ever known. The cauldron was called Oðhrœrir, and the two vats Sôn and Boðn ~ it may only be coincidence, but it is worth marking that these three containers were special enough to receive names, and we have the Irish poem mentioned in Chapter Four referring to the three cauldrons of poetry.

After a few more misadventures, the dwarves were forced to give the mead as a form of *wergild* (blood-money) to a giant. The giant set his unlovely[13] daughter Gunnlauth to guard the mead in a cave. Odin himself determined to bring Kvasir's blood back to the Gods and, through assorted trickery and cunning, transformed himself into an eagle and flew off with the mead in the pouches of his cheeks (if such an undignified thing can be imagined of an eagle, flapping about like a feathered hamster). With the furious giant Suttung in hot pursuit, Odin came in sight of Asgard, where the other gods had set out pots, cauldrons, gazundas and jars to hold the vast amount of mead. He managed to spit most of it into the containers, but some splattered down in droplets to Midgard ~ the land of humankind. Where the drops landed on people, they gained poetic powers and inspiration. The gods have spat upon poets, and not for the first time!

Poetry then, is as intoxicating as mead, as sweet as bee-gold, a precious gift from the gods to mortal kind. Whether the Christian scribe who recorded it at all influenced this story, I do not know, but there are striking similarities between transubstantiation and the notion of mead being, in part, holy blood.

The professional Heathen poets of former times were called skalds and *scops*, and their services in reciting long poems and composing words of praise about heroes and kings were much sought after. They held the same kind of position in Scandinavian and Germanic societies that the bards and *filidh* did in Celtic lands. The songs and stories of the *scops* were magical (much as with the bards and *filidh*), and their name shares a root with the verb "to shape" ~ it may be conjectured that they were able to shape the world around them by singing and speaking aspects of it into existence. The same idea is magnificently captured in the Ancient Egyptian tradition of *heka*, spoken magic, whereby the world is formed and altered by *Netjeru* (deities) correctly enunciating the true spiritual name of things. These true names, or *ren*, are the very essence of the thing named. The goddess Sekhmet did not exist until Re, in a fit of furious disgust at the corruption rife amongst humanity, spoke her name and she leapt fully formed and roaring from his lips.

Frey's True Love – this piece recalls the story of how Frey saw the unusually beautiful giantess Gerð from the vantage point of Odin's throne, and sent his servant to woo her. At first she was terrified of the prospect but, when they finally met, love blossomed. This poem is in Fornyrthislag metre.

Frey's True Love

Falcon's brother stirs	Far-sight in All-Father's seat,
Gymir's daughter golden	Gerð her tapestry tends.
Cold beauty passion brews	Elf lord bends to drink,
Servant summoned	Skivnir sings praises,
Ice hard heart cold	Harsh hall ring disdains.
Idun's gold glitters	Gerð' s apple untasted.
Sword-sharpened curses	Frost shatters, walls weaken.
Nine nights promise	In gnarled woods waits,
Dawn brings dreams delight	Desire fruits in Frey.

The Fish Herd's Words - This piece was written to honour a blót held on a Suffolk beach looking out over the North Sea. It is in Ljóðaháttr metre, a style commonly used for narrative poems ~ especially those intended to be spoken aloud in the first person. The first person in question here is Njord, god of the ocean wave.

The Fish Herd's Words

My hall, my harbour   Good helmsmen meet to feast,
Cold Skadhi scorned these creaking boards for skis,
Frost-bitten and frozen   Frigid Thrymheim's motionless seas,
Water flows, flames flicker, the dance is joy to me.

Loki alone made her laugh   Lurid balls lighten the void,
Gentle Baldur's beauty shook snow from her bough,
Dancing feet delighted   Dire Thiazi's daughter hoped,
A salt-blasted sailor was not her dreaming.

My twisting tides   Her taut ice towers,
Salt melts ice, poor mix for marriage bed,
Yet blizzard winds blow   Bleak the seals domain,
Two houses one bed may still heat.

Sif's Son - A further example of *Ljóðaháttr* metre, this short poem was written for a Winter's Night festival at which the god of winter, Ullr, was honoured with a simple feast. The hunting god is one of the deities by whom oaths were sworn (along with Thor and Frey, with the goddess Vor specialising in marriage oaths).

Sif's Son

Wolf-pawed I prowl.   Past prince of Asgard,
Regaled with rings and wreathed in furs
Oath witness I.   Wild words in winter
By Gunn's mount garnered like gold.

To Vor are vows made;   Sweet vines she tends.
To Thor thoughts flow when duty calls.
Fair Frey follows: Frith 'twixt friends forged,
Wolf's portion is promises made in pain.

Death-deals drawn,   Dire times demand them.
Harken to the howling at Hall's door!
Silence my gift;   Survival your debt,
In the Wolf Age met at winter's edge.

Nehalennia - This short piece was also knocked out for a beach ceremony, a regular occasion held by Suffolk Heathens to honour Nehalennia, the dog-loving goddess of the North Sea who was honoured by Germans, Celts and Romans alike over on the other coast in Zealand.

Nehalennia

Mistress of the Northern Seas
Take ease on your driftwood throne.
Hulls groan, gulls bear merchants pleas
That sweet breeze steer ocean's roan.

Comes the wild and baying hound,
Beach-bound the grey grave-guard laps
Salt strewn paps by shark-home's sound,
Man-meat drowned in sea trolls traps.

Bury their bones in Sea Maid's sand
In Land-Under-Wave they rest,
Sailors nest, till in seals band
They form Her hand, sea-dog's zest.

Apples red from Western Isle
Beguile waves with russet hues
Sun's blood imbues crested mile
Life's dial fades, pays tidal dues.

Shore-side She stands, harbour's Dame
Horizon's aim, boat-bow taught
Travel fraught, oceans ne'er tame
Such a game, adventure wrought!

Hail to Ullr - This poem was composed to honour the god of winter, and read at a blót to mark Yule. Ullr is one of the few Heathen deities with whom I have established a connection (or who has connected to me, depending on point of view), which may be partially due to my obsession with wolves. He has no surviving myths, but I once received one in an inspired moment that has since been retold at gatherings.

Hail to Ullr

Dark and dreaming, deep Ullr's hall,
Its frosted eaves fling shadows far
Shafts on snowfall, shot from ice bow.
Elf-shot melts with morning light bold,
Sun on snow blinds, blazes bow-god eyes
As for the quarry they quest, ice blue.
Oath-Lord takes scent, waits silent for kill.
Knock the bow and beat the heart,
Rhythm of the dance, reason for the draw.

Sif's son patterns Holda's gown with prints
Pursuing prey, he praises her.
Swift death bursts blood on the brightness,
Howls the hunter! Hallow the beast.
Ullr's shield sets sail with its cold cargo,
Sharp bolt slays prey, deep shield sleighs prey.
Fast the wolf to feasting hall fair,
The pack to feed, praise well the dead.

The Fishing Expedition - The following poem relates the story of how Thor nearly defeated the Midgard Serpent, caught after he tricked a giant into taking him for a fishing trip into the depths of the ocean. This somewhat rambling account is in *drottkvaet* metre.

The Fishing Expedition

Hymir's boy manned the oars,
Over fish beds frozen.
Green mountains rose and dropped,
Deadly was Ran's wrath then,
Yet still the colt thrust forth.
Fear stilled great Hymir's heart,
Giant's pleas shatter, fall
Frigid on Thor's false ears.

Anchor weighed, boyish mirth
Marks the deck hand Divine.
Scant the bait, small the hook,
Hymir's haul: limp, lifeless!
Grand the hook, ox-head bait
Bloodies the brine, boy waits...
Sea writhes, roils, serpent coils,
Comes the Midgard monster!

Hel's wyrm howls, fang-swords glint,
Grab the artful angler,
Ducking boy heaves the catch,
Clutches deck, poor purchase.
Muscles strain, swell and bulge,
Boyish guise shed, struggling
Red-beard's rage breaks the hull,
Huge feet firm on sea-bed.

Quaking Hymir wades through
Foul flood, Njord watches, waits.
Earth shudders as the snake
Squirms, bile boils the oceans.
Hand of Asgard's hero
Hammer holds, arcs sky high.
Roars the ancient serpent,
Sunless eyes dreading death.

Thunder brews but slowly,
Silver quick quitter's blade
Before the hammer falls.
Fearful Hymir hacks free
The world-destroying beast
Beneath the tide turns tail.
Thor's blow lands on giant's
Jaw, who sinks to snake's lair.

Thwarted, the angler wades
Wide oceans overcast,
Hammer ploughing trench deep
Ditches, fatal furrows.
Sea beast's nightmares fester,
Fill the deep, doom to man.
Deep thinking Thor waits still,

Sure to slay the reptile.

The Threefold Father – this piece was written for a blót to honour the much-maligned Loki. It is also in *drottkvaet* metre and explores the unusual nature of this deity's role as a parent. Not only was he a father, but also a mother as a result of a gender-swapping experience.

The Threefold Father

Wolf's father, fierce Fenrir's
    Fine sire stands, pack's alpha
Bold howling, blot hallows,
    Heals mead kith, such laughter
Echoes joy, clan's essence
    Endures flame, scorns wasting
Time and wit, Wolf's cunning
    Claims choice meat, guests digest.

Horse mother, sleek Sleipnir's
    Sweet dam dallied, honeyed
Trap tricked, stallion sweated,
    Fair price paid, not too bold
The mare to mask. Manhood?
    Mettle needed, easy
To be bearded, burly,
    Boasting butch. Who bled most?

Corpse father, Helheim's heart,
    Her throne; Death's solace sings
Lullabies. For Loki's
    Lonely girl, loved playmates.
But found fear. Dead daughter
    Delights wights; let Baldur

Shun her not, nor foster
   Feint hearts: live like wildfire!

The Thunderer – this brief verse was written for a blót to honour
Thor. There was an awful lot of sumbl (ritual toasting), which
perhaps explains the warm reception to this otherwise
uninventive piece. Yet more *drottkvaet*, I'm afraid.

The Thunderer

Red-bearded reveller,
   Raid the dark dragon's hoard.
Gold-giver, miser's dread,
   Doom to cold, craven hearts.
Thunder-voiced thane of dwarfs,
   Death-dealer to giants.
Hail the hammer-bearer,
   Bold bright in goat-drawn ship.

Straying away from the Northern Tribes to warmer climes, we
meander into the poetic world of the Mediterranean. I have not,
in fairness, attended a great many Hellenic or Religio Romana
rituals. We used to hold a Lupercalia ritual each February in our
town, though attendance is small (for some reason the prospect
of naked men frolicking in caves with goats and then running
amok in the town seems not to draw many of our local Pagans!)
These days it is basically just me, a wolf skin and a picture of
John Barrowman ~ sad but true.

   There are numerous forms of Greek and Roman poetry. Like
Heathen poetry, the Classical styles did not use end-rhyme.
However, they did not utilise alliteration, like the Germanic
tribes. For them the internal rhythm of syllables was more
important. They recognised six main syllabic combinations,
based upon long sounds and short sounds, practical details of

which may be found in the Appendices (should you wish to try writing in these metres).

The Greeks and Romans honoured Apollon Mousagetēs, that facet of the sun god that lead the Nine Muses and inspired people with the gift of words. The precise number of Muses varied over time, ranging from three to seven to the more widely known Nine. Hesiod described them as daughters of Zeus and Mnemosyne, the goddess of memory, whilst other authors saw them as of titanic origin. The Romans considered their own Camenae goddesses to serve a similar artistic function.

Plato, as recorded in the Phaedrus, considered that there were at least two categories of poetry ~ that divinely inspired by the Muses, and the eminently forgettable product of the human intellect alone:

"And a third kind of possession and madness comes from the Muses. This takes hold upon a gentle and pure soul, arouses it and inspires it to songs and other poetry, and thus by adorning countless deeds of the ancients educates later generations. But he who without the divine madness comes to the doors of the Muses, confident that he will be a good poet by art, meets with no success, and the poetry of the sane man vanishes into nothingness before that of the inspired madmen."

As in so many other cultures, the gift of divine poetry came at a cost ~ the Muses inducing a form of madness along with their gift of memorable poetry. Anyone genuinely able to open their minds to commune with the world of spirits is likely to return from the experience... a tad different!

In the earliest references to them, the Muses were associated with sacred springs ~ the liquid motif seems very widespread; from Kvasir's blood-mead to the three cauldrons, from the potion of Awen and the juices of young Fionn's alfresco roasted Salmon of Wisdom to the waters of the first three Muses.

When writing of the goddess Brigantia in Chapter Two, I mentioned the healing potential of poetry and storytelling. Hesiod said something very similar many centuries earlier, in his Theogeny:

"For though a man have sorrow and grief in his newly-troubled soul and live in dread because his heart is distressed, yet, when a singer, the servant of the Muses, chants the glorious deeds of men of old and the blessed gods who inhabit Olympus, at once he forgets his heaviness and remembers not his sorrows at all; but the gifts of the goddesses soon turn him away from these."

God of Arcady - The poetess Sappho was once greatly revered throughout Greece, and gave her name to a metrical style. This short sample of Sapphic metre is dedicated to that deity so beloved of modern Pagans, and yet so scant regarded by the urbane ancient Hellenes.

God of Arcady

Wild lads dream and play, dancing before Great Pan,
Breeze rich-laden by syrinx sweet, what goat song
Groans honeyed rivulets on my sun wreathed skin?
Noon brings its own risks.

Beasts in silence wait languidly for the Lord
To call the hallowed chorus to howl needful
Praise ~ then the All-Begetter beat his hoofs and
Leads shepherds to lust.

To Antinous - There are various forms of Elegiac Metre, which are used at funerals or in poems marking the demise of a person, age, group or other thing. It's basically a praise poem (rather than a good-riddance-to-you poem) for those in mourning. The style consists of non-rhyming couplets, as many as the poet can be inspired to write.

Upper class Greeks and many Romans idealised the mentoring relationship between and older man and an adolescent just entering Society. Whilst the relationship could be sexualised, it was primarily intended to be didactic and only lasting until the youth became fully adult. Theoretically the two were separated by an age gap of 10 to 15 years, though the Emperor Hadrian was significantly older than his beloved Antinous, with whom he certainly had an erotic, almost obsessive relationship ~ so much so that he never really recovered from the lad's death at age 19. After he drowned in the Nile, Hadrian had the youth apotheosised and temples to the new deity were built all over the Empire. He even had a now-lost Egyptian city named after him, Antinopolis.

In Sparta the younger partner was termed an *aites*, Hearer, and the older an *eispnelas*, Inspirer.

To Antinous

He is lost, Hadrian's beautiful, youthful joy, Nile god gone ~
    sweet child;
Time shall not know him, or carve ownership upon his face,
Raised in rock he is, fixed so men can gaze and lust, beloved
    though doomed
To never grow, never to lead or inspire in his kind.
Peace to his weeping heart, finds worship up on high plinths
    scant solace.
Fire of their Greek love burnt wild heat, such holocaust soon
    cold.

The Final Game – this poem, written in Alcmanian metre, celebrates the Spartan relationship between *aites*, Hearer, and *eispnelas*, Inspirer. Those ferocious warriors of Sparta had, as one of their major annual festivities, a three-day commemoration held at some point in July to honour the apotheosised deity Hyakinthos. This man-god had once been a strikingly handsome warrior prince, much loved by Apollon but also by the spirit of the west wind, Zephyrus. This love triangle ended badly, when the scorned Zephyrus killed the prince during a game of discus throwing. From his blood grew the flowers that still bear his name.

The Spartan festival marked the love, death and resurrection of the prince, an ironic challenge to those who suggest that gays are ill suited to a life in the military! I chose this particular metre because it is named after the first poet known to use it, Alcman of Sparta, whose surviving work includes overtly erotic poetry, written for young women to sing to each other. The Spartans seem to have been remarkably au fait with same-sex love, and it strikes me as an almost Lokean irony that much of his poetry was recovered from an archaeological dig at Oxyrhynchus ~ an Egyptian site sharing its name with the Nile fish that, in the Great Royal Myth, swallowed Asur's severed cock!

The Final Game

So azure those orbs that gazed lovingly at him,
Spartan prince bloomed in spring, season of ardent lust,
Leaf-tender youth's skin sap-sweet as it pined for lips
Stroking and raising stems to strength, how he yearned for
Light ~ such gifts Apollon holds, given free of debts,
Though petals by zephyrs too get touched, no budding
Mind could but be fluttered ~ breeze kissed that heated flesh,
Wooed that lad, noble born, to scant avail. None could
Bright brother to Delos Maiden outshine, West Wind

Paled in buck's sight. Pledges to that glorious God
Died upon youthful lips ~ hated disc stained with blood,
Feeding soil, roots nourished by love lost. Olympus
Grieved. Wrath subdued, blossoms opened – such frail florets,
Fragrance inviting sun's bees to their play, tender
Stars nectar grant, where once Apollon's light they held.

The Wolf Mother – this poem was written for a simple Lupercalia ritual, held on February 15th. In Ancient Rome this festival was considered a bit of a mystery even then, it having been held since time immemorial and continuing well into supposed Christianisation. The name derives from the *lupercal*, the wolf's cave in which the abandoned twins Romulus and Remus were reared by the she-wolf Lupo and her pack. Legend had it that, when the twins were restored to their rightful place in the royal court, they searched out the cave in which they had grown up and, finding the bones of the old wolves, made it into a place of pilgrimage. Each Lupercalia groups of young patrician men gathered at the holy place, stripped off and engaged in rather mysterious rites involving acts of sacrifice. The secretive parts complete, they would then race, nearly naked, round the town trying to impart fertility to the eager young wives of the community by hitting them with skin strips taken from a newly butchered goat. It seems probable that, in its earliest guise, the ceremony was a way for the shepherds to make their peace with local wolf packs. In later times the role of the she-wolf as wet-nurse to Rome itself drew out an element of a Founders Day about the whole event, alongside the official foundation festival on April 21st.

The metre used here is the lesser asclepiad.

The Wolf Mother

Lupo lopes from her cave, eyes glinting deep yellow
Wraith fires writhe, sulphur cage shakes with their rage,
      empty
Cries leap, ghost-breaths mirrors shake in gloom, wolf dives
To the Tiber's banks: two babes, tender, waiting there,
Mars meat lays at her feet, to suckle ~ a god's boon,
He knows a mother true; wild she is this maid of Mars,
Bleached bones broken, her cave no nursery but safe,
Lupo guards head of Rome ~ fate of wolves, chiefs to keep.

[10] There are numerous forms of modern day Druidry, some almost indistinguishable from Christianity or Wicca. They might not find much in common with Heathens, but there is much overlap between the polytheist end of the Druid world and the beliefs and practices of those from the other Northern tribes.

[11] Read *Hitchhikers Guide to the Galaxy*, if you haven't already.

[12] A Heathen term describing an individualised spirit.

[13] Isn't that just an incredibly evocative word? Unlovely... a Widdecombe of a word.

Chapter Six

Here be Kitsch

The following poems are mostly pastiches of more famous and much better works, and were written just for fun or to be annoying (the two often being synonymous, at least for me). What can I say? I'm gay (if you hadn't already guessed from the fey poems about Antinous and Hykinthos); I have a genetic predisposition towards the crass and cheesy. I bake a passable quiche, look divine in fun fur, and go all unnecessary at the sight of John Barrowman[14]. No pontificating about the deep meaning of poetry here, just some nonsense to (hopefully) enjoy.

The Witches Bare Esbat – This piece on nonsense was originally written for the Ipswich Pagan newsletter under the by-line of Miss Cecilia Prim, a little known collector of ditties for Pagan children. It is an unfortunate habit of mine, proving difficult to break, of slipping into multiple personalities whenever the literary mood comes upon me. Miss Prim has acquired a great many dire poems, this being one of the less awful (which gives a sense of how bad the rest must be by contrast).

The Witches Bare Esbat

If you go out in the woods tonight,
You're sure of a big surprise.
If you go out in the woods tonight
You'd better go in disguise.

For every witch that ever there was
Will gather there for certain, because

Tonight's the night the witches bare for their Esbat.

CHORUS ~

Esbat time for witches bare,
Each little witchy bared is having a lovely time tonight.
Watch them, catch them unawares,
And see them frolic at full moon night.
See them Circle-dance about.
They love to drum and shout.
And never have any robes.
At ten o'clock their Lady and Lordy
Will send them home to bed
Because they're tired little Gardnerians.

If you go out in the woods tonight,
You'd better not go alone.
It's lovely out in the woods tonight,
But safer to stay at home.

For every bare old Wiccan there was
Will gather there for certain, because
Tonight's the night the witches bare for their Esbat

CHORUS

Every witchy bare, that's been good
Is flayed with a twig tonight,
There's lots of wonderful mead to swig
And wonderful games to play

Beneath the trees, where nobody sees,
They'll make Great Rite as long as they please,
Tonight's the night the witches bare for their Esbat.

CHORUS

How the Grouch Stole Mithras – a somewhat unfortunate "tribute" to a well-known American children's poem. Apologies to those who prefer the original version! It is a parody, of somewhat dubious historical accuracy, of how an old festival was once borrowed by someone who claimed to know better.

How the Grouch Stole Mithras

Every Rome down in Rome-ana
Liked Mithras a lot
But the Grouch,
Who lived down east of Rome-ana,
Did not!

The Grouch hated Mithras! The whole Mithras cultus!
Now, please don't ask why. He'll just try to insult us.
It could be his faith wasn't held in great light.
It could be, perhaps, that his tomes were full of shite.
But I think that the most likely reason for hate
May have been that his ego was ten sizes too great.

But, whatever the reason,
His ego or his tomes,
He stood there on Mithras' eve, hating the Romes,
Staring down from his cave with a sour, grouchy frown
At the warm lighted windows below in their town
For he knew every Rome down in Rome-ana below
Was busy now, watching for the sun to grow.

"And they're bringing their bullocks!" he snarled with a sneer.
"Tomorrow, Old Mithras, he's practically here!"

Then he growled,
With his Grouch fingers nervously drumming,
"I must find a way to stop Mithras from coming!"
For, tomorrow, he knew
All the Rome lads and maids
Would wake bright and early. They'd rush for their blades!
And then! Oh the blood! Oh the blood! Blood! Blood! Blood!
That's one thing he hated! The blood! Blood! Blood! Blood!

Then the Romes, young and old, would sit down to a feast.
And they'd feast! And they'd feast!
And they'd feast! Feast! Feast! Feast!
They would feast on Rome-vino, and rare wild-roast-boar
Which was something the old Grouch did simply abhor!
And then they'd do something
He hated, those vile brats!

Every Rome down in Rome-ana, the Plebs and the Pats,
Would stand close together, with Mithras bells ringing.
They'd stand hand-in-hand. And the Romes would start
singing!
They'd sing! And they'd sing!
And they'd sing! Sing! Sing! Sing!

And the more the Grouch thought
Of this Rome-Mithras-Sing,
The more the Grouch thought,
"I must stop this whole thing!
"Why, for three hundred years I've put up with it now!
"I must stop this Mithras from coming! But how?"
Then he got an idea!
An awful idea!
The Grouch got a wonderful, awful idea!

"I know just what to do!" The Grouch laughed up a gale.
And he made a quick Messianic mythic tale.
And he chuckled, and clucked, "What a great Grouchy heist!
"In this fanciful book, I sound just like Jesus Christ."
"All I need is a devil"
The Grouch looked around.
But, since devils are scarce, there was none to be found.
Did that stop the old Grouch?
No! The Grouch simply said,
"If I can't find a devil, I'll make one instead!"
So he called Samael. Then he took some red thread
And he tied two big horns on the top of his head.

Then he wrote down some books
Just some old empty sham
On a ramshackle creed
And he hitched up old Sam.
Then the Grouch said, "Hallelujah!"
And the creed started down
Toward the temples where the Romes
Lay a-snooze in their town.

All their windows were dark. Quiet dust filled the air.
All the Romes were all dreaming sweet dreams without care.
When he came to the first little shrine on the square.
"This is stop number one," the old Grouchy Paul hissed
And he climbed to the roof, empty books in his fist.
Then he squeezed through the portal with a fearful slouch.
But, if Lares could do it, then so could the Grouch.

He delayed only once, all timid and wary.
Then he stuck his head into the sanctuary
Where the great Pagan statues all stood in a row.
"These statues," he grinned, "are the first things to go!"

Then he slithered and slunk, like a sleaze from the Senate,
Around the whole shrine, and he took every tenet!
Pontiffs! And pietas! Civitas! Bells!
Festivals! Virgin birth! Priesthood! And smells!
And he stuffed them in books. Then the Grouch, very
cunning,
Stole all the Temples, took over the running!

Then he turned to the rituals. He took the Romes feast!
He took the Rome-vino! He took the roast beast!
He cleaned up the rituals, snuffed their Sacred Fire.
Why, that Grouch even took their vast Roman Empire!
Then he snuffed out the lives of the faithful with glee.

"And now!" grinned the Grouch, "I will chop up the tree!"
And the Grouch grabbed the axe, and he started to hack
When he heard a wild sound like the howl of a pack.
He turned around fast, and saw a fierce Rome!
Great Mater-Lupa Rome, Matriarch of this home.
The Grouch had been caught by this hairy Rome Divine
Who'd heard of an invasion by this sect Pauline.

She stared at the Grouch and said, "Saintly Paul, why?
"Why are you taking our Mithras cult? Why?"
But, you know, that old Grouch was so smart and so slick
He thought up a lie, and he thought it up quick!

"Why, my sweet little maid," the fake holy man lied,
"There's a Truth in this cult that we want on our side.
"So I'm taking it back to the Vatican, dear.
"I'll learn from it there. Then I'll bring it back here."
And his fib fooled the wolf (in truth he preferred sheep...)
And he gave her drugged wine and he put her to sleep.
And when Mater-Lupa Rome went to rest with her cup,

He went to the temple and chopped the tree up!

Then the last thing he took
Was the log for their fire!
Then he went out the temple, himself, the old liar.
In their shrines he left nothing but myths and some fire.
And the one speck of lore
That he left in the shrine
Was a crumb that was even too small to divine.

Then he did the same thing
To the other ancestors.
Leaving crumbs
Much too small
For the future attesters!

It was quarter past dawn
All the Romes quiet indeed,
All the Romes deep a-snooze,
When he packed up his creed,
Packed it up with all their tenets! The temples! The rituals!
The Gods! And the ethics! The legends! The victuals!

Two hundred years more, on the Rock of Saint Peter,
Lupa struggled as the Grouch tried to defeat her!
"Pooh-pooh to the Romes!" he was grouch-ishly humming.
"They're finding out now that Old Mithras ain't coming!
"They're just waking up! I know just what they'll do!
"Their mouths will hang open a minute or two
"Then the Romes down in Rome-ana will all cry boo-hoo!
"That's a noise," grinned the Grouch,
"That I simply must hear!"
So he paused. And the Grouch put his hand to his ear.

And he did hear a sound rising over the dust.
It started in low. Then it started to thrust
But the sound wasn't sad!
Why, this sound sounded merry!
It couldn't be so!
But it was merry! Very!
He stared down at Rome-ana!
The Grouch popped his eyes!
Then he shook!

What he saw was a shocking surprise!
Every Rome down in Rome-ana, the Plebs and the Pats,
Was singing! Sans flamens! Sans creeds! Sans frats!
He hadn't stopped Mithras from coming!
He came!
Somehow or other, he came just the same!

And the Grouch, with his grouch-feet red hot in the sand,
Stood puzzling and puzzling: "How could it be so?
"He came without calling! He came without rites!
"He came without sorcery, candles or lights!"
And he puzzled two millennia, till his puzzler was sore.
Then the Grouch thought of something he hadn't before!
"Maybe Mithras, " he thought, "wasn't made up one day,
"Maybe Mithras perhaps really is here to stay!"

And what happened then?
Well in Rome-ana they say
That the Grouch's huge ego
Shrank three sizes that day!
And the minute his ego didn't feel quite so strong,
He raged and he bellowed from his pulpit long
And he brought back the hate! And the lies and the fear!
And he, he himself!

The Grouch knew his end near!

Bye, Bye Mythological Way - The following classes as filk ~ that is, an existing song whose lyrics have been mangled/rewritten to serve another purpose. Historical purists might object to the disorder sequence of events, but never mind! One of my old university friends, Patricia Taylor, first introduced me to Don McLean, whose song is here shamelessly abused.

Bye, Bye Mythological Way (To the tune of "American Pie")

A long, long time ago
.I remember how the magic used to make me soar
And I wanted to use it well,
Play my part in the Old Gods spell,
And maintain the world like it was afore,
But monotheism made me shiver
With every off'ring I'd deliver,
Bad news in the portents
I couldn't call one more chant
And I can't remember if I cried
When I heard about how Great Pan sighed
But something touched me deep inside
The day the magic died.

CHORUS ~ *So Bye, Bye, Mythological Way,*
Poured out water on the altar, for the altar was dry.
Them harsh ol' priests all started to preach and cry,
singing "Ours'll be the Truth that wont die."

Did we need a book of lore?
We just trusted in the Gods we saw.
Yet now their Bible tells us no!
But I still believe in Gods and wights,

That magic flows during our rites,
And what is there to fear on moonlit nights?
And I know that our old ways were best,
'cause we seized hold of this life with zest,
Yet wise Hypatia's lost,
Cut down by a savage frost.
I was a singer in the temple choir
When the Great Library went right up in fire,
All that knowledge cast on hatred's pyre
The day the magic died
I started singing, bye, bye etc (CHORUS)
For long years we were on our own
Till Julian took the Roman throne
The clock turned back for a brief time.
The Apostate hailed the Gods of Greece
In a robe that whispered "Golden Fleece"
And a voice that down the ages chimes.
And as the king was making good,
Drab Jovian stole his laurel crown,
The revolt was adjourned,
No triumph was returned
As Romans read that book so stark,
The Sun descended in his barque
And we sang dirges in the dark
The day the magic died.
And we were singing, CHORUS
Symmachus spoke like a voice in the wind,
Fat bishops scoffed, and said he had sinned,
Their pet emperor well-trained,
Duly issued his Code
The death-knell for pagans he had sowed.
Snarling Theo, a wolfhound, on his leash strained
Libanius' laments were drowned out,
The Vatican won with a rout,

Temple rubble formed church walls
Filled with the wailing of fools.
Victory's altar cast aside,
No other truth could they abide.
The Vestal Fires were all put out
The day the magic died.

And we were facing one fate,
we found our common ground too late,
with scant time left to save our ways.
Gods were devils, Gods were false,
Gods were just myths (not theirs, of course!)
With carrot and stick there are few that stay,
And so minds were locked in a cage.
My hands were clenched in fists of rage
No saviour born on earth
Could leave us robbed of worth.
And as the axe bit deep into the trees,
Thunor's oak fell to pious sleaze,
Dathi's bough slain, this strange god to please
The day the magic died.

I met a man who knew so much
of dead bones and science and such.
He just smiled like a smug jerk,
I went down to the sacred stone
Where I felt the magic sprite bemoan,
But the man he said the magic wouldn't work
And in the hills the Old Ones slept,
The Druids cried and the bards wept,
But not a word was spoken:
The Church bells all were broken.
For science now reviles its past,
The Church has come full-circle at last

Upon their own rubbish heap cast
The day the magic died.
And we were singing, Bye, Bye, Theological Way,
Bent your halter to the altar, but the altar was clay.
Them harsh ol' priests all started to wail and pray,
singing "Hell 'll be the price that we pay."

Uncle Carbuncle – this story-poem was written as part of a birthday present for my friend, James, who had recently become a father for the first time. I wrote a book of children's stories and poems, so he can read them to young Oscar as he grows into full werewolfhood[15]. The story of Uncle Carbuncle, written in a random metre of my own devising, was inspired partially by a weekend camping trip we had all taken many years earlier to the White Horse of Uffington. Balgan, incidentally, is the name of one of their dogs (a particularly adorable husky).

Uncle Carbuncle

"*Oh dear!*" our Mother said,
Clasping the letter she'd read and re-read,
"*Oh dear, indeed!*" our Father fiercely growled,
As he scowled and re-scowled.
Sister picked up the envelope florid,
Scanned the contents, but found nothing torrid.

Father's glare said it all,
To send such a weird thing ~ what nerve, what gall!
Mauve letters: what would the postman think?
Our fine standing would shrink!
Why was he coming, what could it all mean?
What had stirred up Uncle, so seldom seen?

We looked at each other,

Plucking up courage to ask dear Mother,
"Why, what can it be that causes such woe?"
"Well" she said in tones low,
"Uncle Carbuncle ~ he's coming to stay...
This letter came late ~ he's due here today!"

We fell silent with shock,
Alone could be heard the grandfather clock.
Uncle Carbuncle we'd met once before,
Of him our view was poor.
"Your Mother's brother!" said Father, sniffing,
A sure sign of a forthcoming tiffing.

Out we went with the dog,
To wander the hills obscured by grey fog
Creeping and silent, like Uncle, it coiled.
Up White Horse Hill we toiled.
Each of our steps like a tick on the clock,
Countdown till Uncle's car came in to dock.

By the Horse head we trudged,
Till Balgan sat down and would not be budged,
Our husky threw back his head and howled deep.
Wild panic gripped the sheep!
Down the Horse back Balgan started yanking,
We heard the car come, lurching and clanking.

Fog lights scouring the gloom,
Leaden our steps to avuncular doom.
Aged hearse doors disgorged bloated hop-toad:
Hued-green, eyes-bugged, legs bowed,
Uncle Carbuncle leapt gurgling with glee,
Croaking so loudly we wanted to flee.

At table set for five,
For genteel talk did our poor Father strive
But Uncle babbled of magic and myth,
Father began to sniff,
Mother fretted, but on he talked of spells
And spirits, strange old gods, and fairy bells!

Early we went to bed,
Though sister and I found that sleep had fled.
The clock struck thirteen, and the boards did creak
Downstairs we went to sneak,
And there saw Uncle donning a green cape
"Come with me," he croaked, *"let's have a wild jape!"*

Podgy hand sister took,
She grabbed me too as he, with laughter, shook
"Away, away!" he trilled as the house quaked.
Jade light from his arm snaked,
Hauling us in its wake. We rode the surge
Towards the great Horse Hill, leaping the verge.

To earth we three fools fell,
Sprawled on White Horse back at midnight's last bell.
Midst chalk we rolled, Uncle laughing a gale,
"Here's our mount, seize his tail!"
With that the vast beast galloped, chalk no more ~
Horseflesh sweating, snorting, alive for sure!

"Where are we going?" cried
Sister and I. *"To court me a new bride,
From the Land of the Seelie."* Uncle squealed.
Below moonlight revealed
A wondrous world, where the white horse set down
In dank marsh, near a rickety stilt-town.

"Welcome to fairyland!"
Uncle declared ~ though it seemed far from grand.
No butterfly wings and gossamer wisps,
Or floaty bints with lisps,
Just mud and murk; from the huts Moss Men came:
Warty, webbed and waddling (their Maids the same!)

Their chief laid on a feast,
We dined well till the sun rose in the east.
Out came Anura, daughter of the chief,
Called Uncle her love's thief!
Dreamed of him she had, 'neath the silent moon,
Sickly endearments she began to croon.

Clammy hands grasped, eyes met,
Hearts beat in accord, caught in love's fine net.
Her Knot say: for each toad there is a wart
(They are each other's sort!)
The chief's eyes bugged (well, bugged the more) with rage
To see his spawn fawn over this mere Mage.

Uncle's earnest words failed;
Against mixing pure blood the Moss King railed.
Anura wept, professed that love transcends
All that dark fate intends.
Her brothers menaced us with rusted blades ~
It seemed we three would soon join Pale Death's Shades.

"Epona, Unshoed Queen!"
Our wizard uncle called forces unseen,
Winds swelled, trees groaned, bogs bubbled hungry mire
Moss Men quaked at such ire,
Scattered before the White Horse storming through:
Hauled in its wake, we and the lovers true.

On sky waves riding fast,
Below valleys, woodlands, towns and fields passed.
Like wild salmon to the source we returned,
Exhausted and wind-burned.
Four souls upon the great green hilltop lay,
Listening to dawn's heralds sweet tunes play.

Father baulked at our tale,
Mother met our guest, smiled wan and went pale.
Uncle booked a handfasting for moon's tide,
Kin summoned to meet bride;
Aunts, cousins, grannies came ~ a band most weird
In face, fashion and faith. Poor Father sneered!

Webbed fingers clutched so sweet;
Uncle and Anura like frogs on heat!
Witches and druids whirled in a wild dance.
To taste mead, our first chance
We seized midst cackling crones and wolf-toothed lords;
Whilst our parents hid, we joined with the hordes!

We could have danced all night,
But sleep finally came with heavy might
And we knew no more, till at noon we stirred
As Father brought us word
That the in-laws had gone like morning dew,
Leaving naught but one enormous horseshoe!

[14] Especially when he sings Cole Porter.
[15] It's a long story, but if you live anywhere near Colchester I suggest you avoid going out late at night when the moon is full and unseen things are rustling in the undergrowth.

Anything Goes – every December for the last twelve or more years our Pagan Council has organised a satirical play, almost all of them based on popular plays, films, and books given a Pagan twist. One year we produced a horrifyingly long version of a tale about a young wizard and his experiences at a peculiar school. Keeping with my love of musical theatre (yes, really), a few tuneless pastiches were shoehorned into the plot. One of them, given below, was inspired by my love of the great Cole Porter (I just hope his ghost forgives me). Like other forms of filk, it is intended to be sung ~ preferably off key in a Noel Coward voice.

Anything Goes

In olden days a glimpse of magic
Would lead on to something tragic,
But now, Goddess knows,
Anything goes!

Good Pagans too who once knew ancient myths
Waste lots o' time on silly tiffs,
Bitch-craft grows,
Anything goes!

The world has gone mad today
And pride's bad today,
And truth's trite today,
And lore's "lite" today,
When most Gods today
That Pagans praise today
Are just their own big egos,
And though I'm not a great Arch-druid
I know that sweet mead's the fluid:
Drown our old woes
Anything goes!

When Gerald G whose Craft's not eighty
At moot pubs is now thought weighty by ingénues
Anything goes!

When Heathens pack and leave their old hearths,
Because they decide there's no laughs in Viking shows,
Anything goes!

If hugging great trees you like,
If blessed be's you like,
If old myths you like,
If strange glyphs you like,
If Old Gods you like,
Or eisteddfods you like,
Why, nobody will oppose!
Anything goes!
Anything goes!
Anything goes!

Appendices

Should you wish to have a go at writing some poetry of your own (assuming you don't already do so), then the following advice on metrical construction might prove useful in working with Welsh, Irish and some other metrical forms.

Writing in Irish and Welsh metre

Celtic poetic metres make extensive use of internal and end rhyme, almost like an aural equivalent of the knot work designs that epitomise their artwork. We will begin with a look at how to construct some of the Welsh metres.

Tawddgyrch cadwynog – this form has four-line verses and involves a fair amount of internal rhyme.

Each line has eight syllables.

The rhyme-pattern is shown below, though the positioning of the internal rhyme can shift somewhat.

Some poets split the lines into a series of 4-syllable sentences.

a # # # b
b # # # c
a # # # b
b # # # c

Sample *Tawddgyrch cadwynog* poem:

> *Cafall's stone paw on cairn still seen,*
> *Of dog days proof, the whelp's fame swelled.*
> *The mighty boar for blood was keen,*
> *By Arthur's wean at Cafn felled.*

Englyn Milwr - The easiest of the metres is the Welsh *englyn milwr*, which means soldier's verse. There is no particular guideline as to the sort of theme an englyn can be composed upon.

Each stanza has three lines.
Each line has seven syllables.
The last syllable of each line must rhyme (shown below.)

a
a
a

Sample *englyn milwr* poem:

Lleu's bride, petal soft beauty,
Spills colour rich before me,
To her scent I am a bee

Englyn Cyrch – A straightforward metre this, with a four line verse ~ perhaps a good one for inexperienced poets wanting to experiment.

Each line has seven syllables.
The internal rhyme in the final line can move about (see below).

a
a
b
b # # # a

Sample *englyn cyrch* poem:

Fishguard's fair maid travelled far,
Born along by Druid's car,
From west coast to east she rode,
Paws bestrode, our solstice star.

Cywydd Llosgyrnog - A more complex Welsh metre, which shows the use of internal rhythm, is the *Cywydd Llosgyrnog*. Like the previous example, it has three-line verses. In Welsh poetry triads are very popular.

Lines 1 and 2 both have 8 syllables. Line 3 has 7 syllables.
The last syllable of line 1 rhymes with the last of line 2 and one of the internal syllables (usually the 3rd, 4th or 5th) of line three. Rhyme scheme shown below.
The last syllable of line 3 rhymes with the last syllable of line 3 on the second stanza.

```
# # # # # # a
# # # # # # a
# # a # # # b
        # # # # # # c
        # # # # # # c
        # # c # # # b
```

Sample *Cywydd Llosgyrnog*

White rider of the sacred mounds,
Unleash you pack of grave white hounds
Beyond the bounds of our laws.
    Dark skies rent by the huntsman's flight,
    Arrow flash augurs thunders might,
    In Nudd's height the pale wolf roars.

Englyn Penfyr - A more complex example of internal rhyming is the *Englyn Penfyr* (englyns were most commonly used for praising, cursing or enchanting.)

Each verse has 3 lines.

The first line has 10 syllables, the next two lines have 7 syllables each.

The rhyme scheme is shown below.

```
# # # # # # a # # b
# # # b # # a
# # # # # # a
```

Sample *Englyn Penfyr*

> *The old hunter sought the beast in the night,*
> *Though without might, hope near ceased,*
> *Yet frail, his skill found the feast.*

Englyn Proest Dalgron - Welsh poetry also makes use of half-rhyme. This is a difficult concept to use when writing in English, but a simpler example is the *Englyn Proest Dalgron*.

Each verse has four lines with 7-syllable each.

The end-rhyme is placed upon vowel sounds (bearing in mind that W and Y count as vowels in Welsh), but is only a half-rhyme.

The Welsh divide vowels into two groups ~ long and short sounding. Long vowels are considered to half-rhyme with each other. Likewise short vowels half-rhyme with each other. An example of a long vowel is found in "wood", whilst a short vowel is heard in "wed". Or "tree" (long) and "trip" (short.) More guidance can be found on long and short vowels in the next section on Classical poetic metres. This form of poetry works better in Welsh than it does in English.

```
      # # # # # # a
      # # # # # # a
      # # # # # # a
# # # # # # a
```

Sample *Englyn Proest Dalgron*:

> *The yew has a rare berry*
> *Which to death leads, like the sow*
> *Hen Wen, devourer of Lleu.*
> *The dark seed for which we die.*

Irish poetry also places emphasis on end- and internal-rhyme. Unlike Welsh poetry, Irish verses must be cyclical (something which I haven't always stuck to in the poems given in this book). This means that the very last syllable of the whole poem must rhyme with the very first. The technique is called a *dunadh,* and some poets simply repeat the entire first sentence. This final rhyme takes place regardless of the demands of the rhyme scheme of the last verse.

Ae Freisilighe - A sample Irish metre is the *Ae Freisilighe* that, like most Irish poetry, is made up of four-line verses.

Each verse has four lines. There are seven syllables to a line.
The 1st and 3rd lines must end on a 3-syllable word.
The 2nd and 4th lines must end on a 2-syllable word.
However, it is only the final syllable of each line that need rhyme, not the whole word.

```
      # # # # (# # a)
      # # # # (# b)
```

```
# # # # (# # a)
# # # # # (# b)
```

Sample *ae freisilighe* verse:

> *Through mists writhing, Manannán*
> *Leaps joyous, mind in wonder*
> *At all, from dark Cruachain*
> *To shell-bright sea vast plunder.*

Rannaigheacht Mór - Another example of an Irish quatrain (four-line verse) is the *rannaigheacht mór* whose format is as follows.

Each verse has four lines, each line has seven syllables.

The end-rhyme of the third line has an internal rhyme (called an *aicill*) within the fourth line.

The last two words of the fourth line should alliterate.

```
# # # # # # a
# # # # # # b
# # # # # # a
# # a # # # b (last two words alliterate)
```

Sample *rannaigheacht mór* poem:

> *Goat-hoofed Pooka, feathered, furred,*
> *Twists and turns about the field*
> *Where the bounds of flesh are blurred,*
> *Mirth oft stirred, sorrow's storm stilled.*

Deibhidhe – A quatrain that, technically, should involve specific use of stressed and unstressed syllables. However, I suggest that inexperienced poets (or lazy ones, like me) ignore the stress rules given below until they are more confident at composing.

Each line has seven syllables

The odd lines should end in stressed syllables, the even ones with unstressed ones.

The last word in each verse should alliterate with the previous stressed word (a difficult one this, perhaps this aspect is best left until you have got the gist of writing in the general metrical format first).

The rhyme scheme is as follows below.

```
# # # # # # a
# # # # # # a
# # # # # # b
# # b # # # b
```

Sample *deibhidhe* verse:

> *Wolves walked here once, silent paws*
> *Tracked prey across forest floors.*
> *Howling circled blessed isle,*
> *Lupine guile countered Man's bile.*

Writing in Heathen metre

Heathen poetry does not usually rhyme on the final word of each line, but relies on phonetic alliteration ~ words that begin with the same consonant sounds (even if they're not spelt the same way.) A straightforward alliteration would be: "*The red rooster runs.*" A more complex example would be: "*Phosphorous fire filled the cave.*" The "ph" and "f" alliterate because they sound alike.

In strict Icelandic poetry some letters that we class as consonants they class as vowels, but as this is a basic poetry class we will ignore that for now! Note that digraphs (two consonants conjoined together, like "th" or "sk") need to alliterate with other words starting with the same digraph or a similar sound. For example, tripe alliterates with trinity, but not with turnip; whilst sheep alliterates with shine, and also with sugar (because of the phonetics).

Drottkvaett (Courtly / Lordly Metre)

Each stanza consists of eight lines. Each line should have six syllables.

Lines 1, 3, 5, & 7 should each contain two or three alliterating words.

Lines 2, 4, 6, & 8 should ideally contain some assonance and/or internal rhyme (if you can squeeze it in.) The first word of each of these lines should alliterate with the last word of the previous line.

Ideally the last word of each line should have two syllables, the first long and the second short (e.g. *deepen, horseman, sheepish, warden.*)

Even more ideally, the last word of line 4 should be the end of a sentence.

A variant form of *drottkvaett* follows the above rules but has eight syllables in each line. This metre is called *hrynhenda*.

Sample *drottkvaett* poem:

> *Raedwald's wife knew reason,*
> *Regal shield, Frig's eagle.*
> *Staunch strategic counsel,*
> *Kind words for hostages.*
> > *Altars honoured always,*
> > *Astride two worlds rides she,*

Bede bore her but meanly,
Maid robbed of name, not fame.

Fornyrthislag - Old Metre. There is some evidence that this style of metre was used for storytelling, recounting poems about myths and legends. It does make for a good metre in which to recite a tale.

Each stanza has four lines, all of which are half-lines (have a natural pause.)

Each half should have two emphasised syllables (and two or three unaccented syllables). One of the emphasised syllables in the first half should alliterate with the first emphasised syllable of the second half, but NOT the final emphasised syllable at the end of the poem.

A sample *fornythislag* poem:

Red bearded reveler	*Deep resting at Hall*
All-wise comes calling	*A cold comfort for Thrud*
Wooed by forge spark	*He spoke much*
Till dawn light crept	*Deathly silence ensued.*

Ljóðaháttr - Song Metre. There is some evidence that this style of metre was used for poems spoken by a character in the first person, such as a god or hero talking about what they have done.

A stanza consists of four lines ~ alternating between full lines and half lines.

The odd numbered half-lines have a natural pause and two accented (emphasised) syllables in either half;

A word from the first part of the half-line must alliterate with the first emphasised syllable in the second part of the half-line;

The even numbered lines have no pause, three accented

syllables of which either two or all three alliterate.

A sample *ljóðaháttr* poem:

> *Glitnir's gold oversees all*   *Gilds the laws therein.*
> *Twelve men molded me*
> *On the holy isle.*   *Harmony flowed forth*
> *As I silenced the law-lords.*

Writing in Classical metre

Like Heathen poetry, the Classical styles did not use end-rhyme. However, they did not utilise alliteration, like the Germanic tribes. For them the internal rhythm of syllables was more important. They recognised six main syllabic combinations, based upon long sounds and short sounds.

Examples of long syllables are: *hay, pain, seed, weak, eye, time, Rome, cope, huge, loop, wound etc.*

Examples of short syllables are: *cat, ram, elf, pelt, it, wing, of, rope, up, shut etc.*

The six combinations:

Iambus	S - L	eg	*Neptune*
Trochee	L - S	eg	*Flora*
Spondee	L - L	eg	*Juno*
Pyrrhic	S – S	eg	*Vulcan*
Anapest	S - S - L	eg	*Hecate*
Dactyl	L - S - S	eg	*Diana*

The poetess Sappho was once greatly revered throughout Greece, and gave her name to a metrical style that you can experiment with. Each verse is four lines long, and combines various types of syllabic measure. Remember, you don't need to rhyme the lines, simply stick to the combination of short and long vowels.

Sapphic Metre

L - S - L - S - L - S - S - L - S - L - S
L - S - L - S - L - S - S - L - S - L - S
L - S - L - S - L - S - S - L - S - L - S
L - S - S - L - S

Sample Sapphic verse:

> *Wisest sage, born amongst scrub ~ basest beasts penned*
> *By their own lusts. Four legged sons by the rain clouds*
> *Sired, but Chiron came from much nobler breed stock,*
> *Teacher of great men.*

There are various forms of Elegiac Metre, which are used at funerals or in poems marking the demise of a person, age, group or other thing. It's basically a praise poem (rather than a good-riddance-to-you poem!) The style consists of non-rhyming couplets, as many as the poet can be inspired to write.

Elegiac Metre

L - S - S - L - S - S - L - S - S - L - S - S - L - S - S - L - L
L - S - S - L - S - S - L - L - S - S - L - S - S - L

Sample elegiac verse:

Time ends and silence falls, the Doctor's bright tenancy terminates, weep
Angels, blink those salt tears away ~ give him smiles not sorrow.

Alcmanian metre is credited to the Spartan poet Alcman, who wrote pieces for choirs to sing. He was known for his light, at times humorous, touch. Again, there was no expectation of rhyme, the emphasis being placed on syllabic length instead. An alcmanian line is paced as shown below, and a verse can contain any number of them.

Alcmanian metre

L – S – S – L – S – S – L – S – S – L – S – S

Grapes hang pendulous, ready for death, bleeding joy:
Freedom for minds boxed in by dignity ~ nectar!

Lesser asclepiad metre is credited to the erotic poet Asclepiades of Samos. There is also a greater asclepiad metre, similar in style to the one used here but slightly longer. An asclepiad line is paced as shown below, and a verse can contain any number of them.

Lesser asclepiad metre

L – L – L – S – S – L – L – S – S – L – S – L

Night reigns, heat stirs his veins to pulse, lids open wide,
He smiles, my lips wet, part, respond with sleeper's hope.
Need grows, tasting of seaside holidays: salt-sweet
Beneath the sun, where seas hide hungers rising at

Moon tide to walk upon beaches where sailors dream.

A Brief Glossary of Poetic Jargon

Alliteration   The repetition of the same consonant sounds. Example ~ *The fiery fox fell in the flames.*

Assonance   The repetition of the same vowel sounds. Example ~ *Flee by sea in a reed boat.*

Rhyme   The repetition of the same vowel and consonant sounds. Example ~ *The fat cat fell splat from the flat window.*

End-rhyme   As above, but the syllables that rhyme are the last ones in each line.

Internal rhyme   The end syllable of one line usually rhymes with a word appearing somewhere in the middle of another line.

Kenning   Spiritual or magical metaphors, popular throughout many Pagan cultures. Examples ~ *The horses of Manannan* (waves of the sea); *Old One Eye* (Odin); *The Eternal City* (Rome)

Recommended Reading

Bergin, Osborn, *Irish Bardic Poetry*, Dublin Institute, Dublin, 1984 reprint, ISBN – 9780901282125

Carmichael, Alexander, *Carmina Gadelica*, Floris Books, Edinburgh, 1992 reprint, ISBN – 0863155200

Herne, Robin, *Old Gods, New Druids*, 0 Books, Winchester, 2009, ISBN – 9781846942266

Jackson, Kenneth, *Studies in Early Celtic Nature Poetry*, Llanerch Publishers, Lampeter, 1995 reprint, ISBN – 1897853793

Kinsella, Thomas, *The New Oxford Book of Irish Verse*, Oxford University Press, Oxford, 1989, ISBN – 0192801929

Lofmark, Carl, *Bards and Heroes*, Llanerch Publishers, Lampeter, 1989 reprint, ISBN – 0947992340

Meyer, Kuno, *Fianaigecht*, Dundalgan Press, Dublin, 1993 reprint, ISBN – 1855001721

Ó Searchaigh, Cathal, *By the Hearth in Mín a' Leá*, Arc Publications, Todmorden, 2005 ISBN – 1904614213

Skelton, Robin, *Samhain*, Salmon Poetry, Dublin, 1994, ISBN – 1897648138

Moon Books invites you to begin or deepen your encounter with Paganism, in all its rich, creative, flourishing forms.